Birds of
the Eastern Caribbean

Peter G H Evans

Edward Grey Institute, Department of Zoology,
University of Oxford, England

First published 1990 by
MACMILLAN EDUCATION LTD
London and Basingstoke
*Associated companies and representatives in Accra, Banjul,
Cairo, Dar es Salaam, Delhi, Freetown, Gaborone, Harare,
Hong Kong, Johannesburg, Kampala, Lagos, Lahore, Lusaka,
Mexico City, Nairobi, São Paulo, Tokyo*

ISBN 0–333–52155–2

15	14	13	12	11	10	9	8	7	6
05	04	03	02	01	00	99	98	97	96

Printed in Hong Kong

A catalogue record for this book is available from the
British Library.

Contents

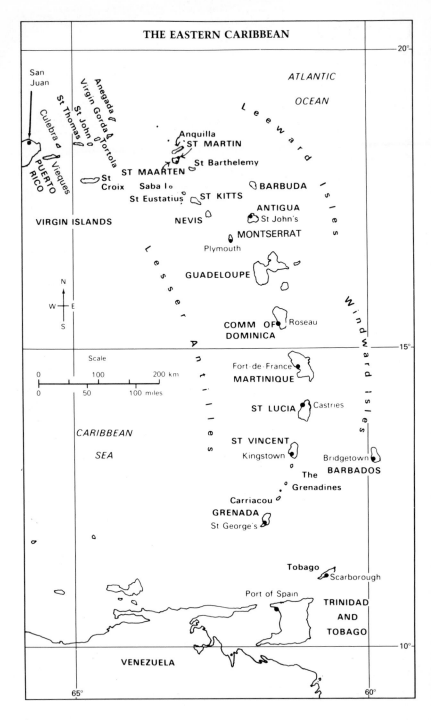

THE EASTERN CARIBBEAN

ATLANTIC

OCEAN

San
Juan

Anegada

Virgin Gorda

St John

Tortola

St Thomas

Culebra

PUERTO
RICO

Vieques

VIRGIN ISLANDS

St
Croix

Leeward isles

Anquilla
ST MARTIN

ST MAARTEN

St Barthelemy

Saba I o

St Eustatius

ST KITTS

BARBUDA

NEVIS

ANTIGUA
St John's

MONTSERRAT

Plymouth

Lesser

GUADELOUPE

N
W—E
S

COMM OF
DOMINICA

Roseau

Antilles

Windward isles

Scale

0   100   200 km

0   50   100 miles

Fort-de-France
MARTINIQUE

CARIBBEAN

SEA

ST LUCIA

Castries

ST VINCENT

Kingstown

The

Grenadines

Bridgetown

BARBADOS

Carriacou

GRENADA

St George's

Tobago

Scarborough

Port of Spain

TRINIDAD

AND

TOBAGO

VENEZUELA

20°

15°

10°

65°

60°

iv

Preface

This book treats 180 species of birds that either breed in or regularly visit the islands of the Eastern Caribbean, from the Virgin Islands to Grenada. There is a brief introduction to the birds of the region followed by short sections on features of the breeding biology and ecology that characterise Eastern Caribbean birds, including the habitats in which they live. Some hints are then given on how to get the best out of bird-watching and from bird photography. This is followed by a section on conservation. The main substance of the book is devoted to brief accounts of all the breeding species and the commoner migrants/visitors. Within a family, species are arranged for ease of comparison between those that are similar in appearance. Each species has a brief description with emphasis on key identification features, a review of its status, distribution and habitat, and aspects of its breeding biology, diet and behaviour. All the commoner species are illustrated by a colour photograph. Where the male and female of a species differ markedly in appearance, both are depicted. The great majority of pictures were taken in the Eastern Caribbean but emphasis is given to the selection of photographs which best show the main features of the species. For this reason some close-up photographs of hand-held birds are included in preference to field shots.

A list of the 145 breeding species (including exotics) and 143 non-breeding migrants and winter visitors (omitting vagrants recorded only once in recent times) forms an appendix at the end of the book. Finally there are two further appendices, one listing some of the best bird-watching places by island/island group, and the other a select bibliography to enable the reader to follow up his/her interest in an area in more detail.

Acknowledgements

In preparing this short guide, I should like to thank the following colleagues for so kindly reviewing sections or providing unpublished and published material: Wayne Arendt, David Blochstein, Paul Butler, John Faaborg, Ruud van Halewyn, Morris Hutt, Robert Norton and Herbert Raffaele. I also thank my friends and colleagues in Dominica for their continued support over the years during my own research there. These include in particular Christopher Maximea and Felix Gregoire and their staff in the Forestry Division, Marshall and Loye Barnard, Duane Bush, the Honychurch and Astaphan families. Finally those studies would not have been possible without the sterling efforts of many participants and the funding support of the International Council for Bird Preservation and other conservation-minded organisations.

The author and publishers wish to acknowledge, with thanks, the following photographic sources:
Ardea: p 121 (top) Edgar T. Jones; p 127 (bottom) M.D. England; p 27 (right) Francois Gohier
M. de L. Brooke: p 17 (bottom); p 21 (bottom left)
S.T. Buckton: p 84 (left)
P. Butler: p 76 (top right and bottom)
T.A. Carlo: p 70 (right)
J.A. Colon: p 39; 47 (top right and bottom); 49 (right); 50 (left); 54 (top right); 58 (right); 69 (left); 79 (right); 111 (top)
M. Garnett: p 66 (bottom)
M.P. Harris: p 21 (top left); 21 (top right); 21 (bottom right); 23 (left); 25 (right); 50 (right); 66 (top)
E. Hernández: p 101 (right)
G. Hirons: p 29 (right); 82
P. Robertson: 101 (left); 115 (bottom left)
Other photographs by P.G.H. Evans

Introduction

Contained entirely within the latitudes of 10 and 20 degrees north lie the islands of the Eastern Caribbean. They stretch in an arc from the Virgin Islands in the north-west to Trinidad and Tobago in the south (see map page iv). Excluding those islands, they form the chain known as the Lesser Antilles, volcanic mountain peaks uplifted to fifteen hundred metres above the sea with an outer, older arc to the east comprising low limestone platforms, the caps of ancient, submerged volcanoes. In geology, the Virgin Islands belong to the cordillera of the Greater Antilles, but they share many features of the avifaunas of the Lesser Antillean islands and so will be treated accordingly here. On the other hand, Trinidad and Tobago, lying only 16 km (10 miles) from the mainland of Venezuela have a distinctly continental South American avifauna with over 400 species recorded. They have formed the subject of a companion volume by Richard ffrench and so will not be considered further in this book.

Although some of the islands contain a few bird species occurring only on that island (referred to as endemic), many species may be found throughout the region. Differences in avifaunas between islands are the result of a combination of factors: island size and height above sea level, habitat variety, isolation, and the impact of humans and various introduced animals. These influences are considered in a little more detail in later sections.

Over 350 species (288 + at least 64 vagrants/unestablished exotics) of birds have been recorded in the Eastern Caribbean region (excluding Trinidad and Tobago). Many of these are North American migrants. Between July and November, songbirds particularly parulid warblers from the woods of the United States, and shorebirds (sandpipers, dowitchers, yellowlegs and the like) from as far north as Arctic Canada, migrate southward through the Caribbean to winter in South America. These islands form important resting places where the birds can feed up before continuing their long journey south. The following spring, from January to April, those birds return, although they tend to spend less time in the Caribbean during this migration, hurrying onward to their North American breeding grounds. Some species remain in the region throughout the winter rather than using the area temporarily for migration. Other birds also visit the Lesser Antilles

1

between autumn and spring. These include raptors such as merlin and peregrine, and waterfowl such as blue-winged and green-winged teal. 134 species are known presently to breed in the region.

ECOLOGY

The islands of the Caribbean contain a rich variety of habitats ranging from cloud forest and elfin woodland along the mountain tops, through rain forest to coastal thicket and dry scrub woodland, mangrove swamp and marshes, rugged sea-cliffs and coral cays. This range of habitats results from variation in geology and topography, and the influence this has upon the local climate. As the prevailing easterly winds from the Atlantic meet the peaks of the more mountainous Antillean islands, the clouds laden with moisture from the forests beneath are forced upwards where they cool, giving rise to heavy rains which fall throughout most of the year. On the leeward Caribbean coasts of these islands, the land lies in the rain shadow of the mountains. Here, the climate is dry

Littoral woodland

Dry scrub woodland interior

Mangrove swamp

3

and seasonal, with little rainfall between the months of January and June. The vegetation is adapted to long spells without rain. Many plants are deciduous, shedding their leaves in the dry season, their leaves are usually small with thick cuticles and their trunks or branches possess spines. In these dry, often open coastal woodlands live birds that feed particularly on insects or nectar from flowering trees and shrubs, species such as flycatchers and hummingbirds, yellow warblers and bananaquits. Seed-eaters are also well represented with ground-feeding doves and finches such as bullfinch, grassquit and streaked saltator. Many of the marshes and mangrove swamps are to be found in coastal areas and these are haunts of herons and egrets, ducks, wintering belted kingfisher, various rails and gallinules, with waders along exposed mudflats or damp meadows. Boobies, tropic birds and several species of terns may be found nesting along cliffs and on small islands that are relatively inaccessible to humans who exploit them for eggs and meat.

Some of the lower-lying islands such as Antigua, Barbados and the Virgin Islands have lost most if not all of their natural habitat

Swamp vegetation

to cultivation and these areas generally share the same assemblage of birds of secondary habitat. Carib grackles and tropical mocking-birds feed on pastures along with anis and cattle egrets. In damper meadows these are often joined by little blue and green-backed herons. Sugar (and cotton) plantations have little to offer in the way of birdlife except the ubiquitous bananaquit, bullfinch and grassquit, green-throated and Antillean crested hummingbirds. These species, along with the shiny cowbird and yellow grass finch on some islands, are also the ones most frequently observed in parks and gardens. Plantations of banana, citrus and coconut are better, so long as they are interspersed with other trees or shrubs, native species and crops such as coffee, cacao, mango and pawpaw. These plantations are traditionally used by tyrant flycatchers, thrashers and saltators, and larger birds such as pigeons and doves, and the American kestrel may visit those with high canopies.

Much of the evergreen rain forest that covered the interior of the larger islands has now been cleared by humans. Only the islands of Dominica, Guadeloupe, Martinique and St Vincent have extensive tracts remaining, although small areas of good forest

Rain forest

Rain forest interior

occur in St Lucia, St Kitts, Montserrat and Grenada. It is in these areas that many island endemics (species confined to an island or island group) can be found: all the *Amazona* parrots (Dominica, St Lucia, and St Vincent), orioles (Montserrat, Martinique and St Lucia), Guadeloupe woodpecker, and species such as the forest thrush (Dominica, Guadeloupe, St Lucia, and Montserrat), plumbeous warbler (Dominica and Guadeloupe), and blue-headed hummingbird (Dominica and Martinique).

Higher up in the mountains, the rain forest gives way to montane thicket, palm brake, and elfin woodland (cloud forest of stunted height), and the canopy height of 30 – 35 metres becomes reduced to a mere 3 metres where the tangled branches of *Clusia* dominate the elfin woodland of the ridges and more exposed slopes. This is

Montane thicket and swamp

Elfin woodland vegetation

the domain of the rufous-throated solitaire, known locally as the mountain whistler or siffleur montagne, and on those particular islands where they occur, the house wren, plumbeous warbler and blue-headed hummingbird are most abundant here.

Many tropical plants produce showy flowers or fruits that are attractive to birds. These provide important food in the form of nectar for hummingbirds and bananaquits, and fleshy fruits for pigeons and parrots, thrushes, thrashers, finches and flycatchers. By feeding upon them, many birds also serve an important role for the plants by aiding their pollination or dispersal of their seeds. Different plants may flower or fruit at different times of the year so that some food is available to the birds in every month. In this way, birds and plants have evolved together to their mutual benefit. If one were removed this would have a detrimental effect upon the other, a feature that is often overlooked in the Caribbean when considering conservation of its wildlife and the forests in which they live. Many Caribbean birds are very opportunistic in their diet. We tend to think of flycatchers, warblers and vireos as being insectivorous but in this region they will also feed upon small fruits when they are available. Conversely, thrushes and thrashers that are primarily frugivorous (fruit-eating) will also feed upon insects.

The number of breeding species upon an island depends to a great extent upon the size of that island and the variety of habitats it has. Bigger islands usually have a wider range of habitats of a reasonable size. For this reason, it is the larger islands that have the most bird species. The richest of all habitats tends to be rain forest, so the best avifaunas are to be found on those islands such as Dominica with the most undisturbed forest. Islands that are close to a rich source of immigrants will also have richer avifaunas. Thus, Trinidad and Tobago lying so close to the South American mainland, have been colonised by a great many species from the continent. The Virgin Islands and other Greater Antillean islands have received a relatively large number of immigrants from North America. Those islands in the centre of an island chain are relatively isolated and so have fewer colonists. On the other hand, this comparative isolation tends to give rise to species that are not to be found on any other island. All but the smallest Lesser Antillean islands have at least one endemic bird species, Dominica and St Vincent having two and St Lucia four (though one of these may now be extinct). The Lesser Antillean islands tend to have been colonised by species from South America, and it is likely that regular hurricanes coming from the south, have been responsible for many such colonisations.

BREEDING BIOLOGY

One of the most important features of the tropics is the absence of distinct seasons. Temperatures fluctuate little throughout the year and although along the leeward coasts there is a definite dry season sometime during the first six months, its timing may vary from year to year, whilst in the interior of the more mountainous islands, rainfall is only slightly reduced usually for less than 3 or 4 months in the year. This lack of strong seasonality means that many bird species (for example hummingbirds, bananaquits, bullfinches and grassquits) may breed several times through the year. The rest for the most part breed during the middle of the dry season, particularly from February to May.

Compared with the mainland counterparts, Lesser Antillean birds lay slightly smaller clutches of eggs, perhaps because there is no strong peak in food abundance during the time of chick rearing to support more young as occurs in temperate regions. On the other hand, most species appear to have a higher survival rate and to be relatively long-lived. It is thought that in a tropical environment, birds are less likely to die of cold or food shortage, instead being more vulnerable to predation.

Shortly after the breeding season, the majority of species moult their wing feathers followed by the tail and body feathers. In some species (for example grassquit), they may start a moult then suspend this to breed before continuing again after the young have fledged.

Most Caribbean birds nest solitarily, often building cup-shaped or domed nests with a small side entrance for protection from predators. Exceptions are the colonial seabirds, many herons and egrets. Carib grackles may also nest colonially in small groups, their pendulous nests commonly hanging from palms or pine trees. The related shiny or glossy cowbird is parasitic and lays its eggs in the nests of other species in the same way as some cuckoo species. Sometimes several females may lay in the same nest. Smooth-billed anis do likewise but in the nests of their own species. They live in family groups and several related females help one another to build a large nest into which they lay their eggs. They then co-operate in incubating the eggs and, once these hatch, they collectively feed the young. Rather little is known about the mating systems of other Caribbean birds. Some species form what are known as leks, where several males come together in the same area to compete for one or more females. Those include hermit hummingbirds and manakins of Trinidad and Tobago. Species that compete in this way are usually polygynous, in other words one male may mate with more than one female over a short period. The bananaquit may also be polygynous. If a female deserts her nest early in the season (for example after predation of her eggs), she may then leave her mate and settle with another already mated male.

BIRD-WATCHING

The visitor to the West Indies does not face the same bewildering array of species that he or she would meet on the South American mainland, so that identifying birds should not be a great problem. Closely related species that are similar in appearance are usually not found together on the same island so that potential identification difficulties rarely occur. Nevertheless, there are a number of suggestions one can make that should help the visitor to get the most out of bird-watching in these islands.

If the stay is a long one, then visit as many different habitats as possible from sea cliff, swamp and lake, garden and parkland, to dry forest, rain forest and mountain top. This should maximise the number of different species to be seen. Particularly in dry areas, there is a distinct lull in activity amongst birds in late morning through early afternoon. At this time the sun is at its highest and most birds are resting in the shade. Peak activity is generally in the first three hours after dawn and the last two to three hours before dusk so these are the best times to bird-watch.

Although not necessarily shy or retiring, birds in the Caribbean can best be watched by sitting still and allowing them to come to you, or by making all movements slow and quiet. This applies particularly within the rain forest where birds otherwise are difficult to detect except from the sounds that they make. Indeed, forest birds are much more readily heard than seen, and bird-watchers are recommended to learn the different calls and songs they make. Between January and May in the earlier part of the breeding season of most species, there is often a peak in song, although some species such as the solitaire may sing at any time of the year. The songs of each species are usually distinctive but the same is not the case for many calls. Thus a ticking or chucking sound may be made by house wren and plumbeous warbler, pearly-eyed and scaly-breasted thrasher, and forest thrush whilst a not dissimilar alarm note is made by all the hummingbird species, bananaquit and bullfinch. Differences between each can be quite subtle, involving variation in pitch or repetition rate.

When an unfamiliar bird is seen, it is wise to make detailed notes.

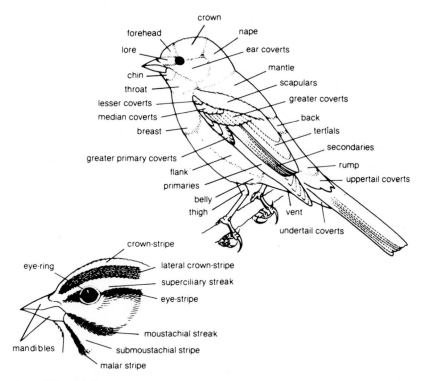

Describing birds

Record its size, general shape and posture, length of bill and of tail, coloration and special markings, presence of eye-stripes or bars on the wing or tail. Behaviour also provides important clues to identity. Does the bird hover or glide when flying? Is the flight direct or undulating? How does the bird perch? Is it a ground dweller or does it sit high in the canopy? Does it glean insects off leaves or flycatch by short forays into the air? These are just some of the questions which should also be considered in the short time that the bird may be in view. Remember also to make notes as soon after the sighting as possible as one's memory can readily play tricks, and a later perusal of an illustrated field guide may influence your decision on what actually was seen.

A pair of binoculars, though not essential, is an important aid both in searching for birds and trying to identify them. Any magnification between 7 and 10× is appropriate. The higher the value, the greater the magnification but with this generally comes greater size and weight, a narrower field of view and poorer light-gathering power. Thus although binoculars of 7× magnification

11

are not as powerful as $10\times$, they usually give a much brighter image and the field of view is larger so that birds can be better located amongst foliage. Less than $7\times$ tends to be too weak a magnification whereas greater than $10\times$, the quality and resolution of the image usually diminishes greatly.

For viewing birds on mud-flats, across swamps or large water masses, or on sea-cliffs, a telescope is a useful additional item of equipment. The magnification may vary from 20 to $60\times$, bearing in mind that a greater power tends to be offset by poorer resolution. Furthermore, in the tropics there is often a heat haze, the effects of which are particularly noticeable at higher magnifications. In the Caribbean, I rarely use an objective greater than $20\times$ on my telescope. Most important, however, is to have a solid tripod on which to mount the telescope. A steady base makes a great difference to the ease with which one can make out detail at a distance, particularly with higher magnifications.

PHOTOGRAPHY

It is usually possible to approach birds in the Caribbean sufficiently closely to photograph them without a hide so long as one has a reasonably powerful telephoto lens (300 mm or above). However, always put the bird first and avoid taking pictures at the nest. The single most difficult factor to overcome is light. It is surprising how little light there is amongst trees and foliage, and a high speed film (minimum of 200 or 400 ASA) is recommended. An electronic flash may also be necessary under certain circumstances. If a telephoto lens is being used then it is wise to mount it on a pistol grip or some other form of tele grip, or alternatively upon a firm tripod. Use a fast shutter speed (1/250 second or above).

Many birds can be attracted to a bait such as rotting bananas or grapefruit, and hummingbirds tend to visit the same flowers repeatedly during a morning so that one can sit in wait for them. They are rarely troubled by human presence so long as one is quiet and does not move around. In those cases, a long telephoto is often not necessary, but a macro zoom lens such as of focal length 70 – 210 mm can be useful since it provides one with some flexibility and allows one to approach several species, particularly the hummingbirds, to within a metre or so.

Heat and high humidity are two ever present dangers facing the photographer in the Caribbean and both equipment and films should be stored in a cool, dry place, preferably in containers of silica gel to remove moisture. Once exposed, films should be sent for processing reasonably quickly as the colour balance can be readily affected by heat if stored.

CONSERVATION

The islands of the Eastern Caribbean are very different places to what they were five hundred years ago when Christopher Columbus brought the first Europeans to the region. At that time, although Arawak and then Carib Indians had been living on the islands for over a thousand years, most of the land was probably still thickly forested, settlement being confined primarily to the coast. With the arrival of Europeans together with peoples from West Africa, this changed dramatically at least on the lower, less rugged islands. Successions of plantation crops have denuded many of the islands of their natural vegetation, reducing this to isolated patches of scrub. Coastal woodlands in particular were often greatly reduced in area and it is likely that a number of bird species, once occurring on the Lesser Antilles, became extinct during those centuries following colonisation. Only the larger, more mountainous islands have retained extensive tracts of forest and now these face further threats from development.

Habitat loss is undoubtedly the major threat to Caribbean birds; most endangered species are under threat from habitat loss alone or from habitat loss combined with other factors such as predation from introduced animals, or collection for the pet trade. Several species now face extinction. There are only about sixty pairs of white-breasted thrasher left on St Lucia, whilst in the same island, the endemic Semper's warbler has only been recorded four times in the last forty years. All four endemic parrots are endangered, with only about sixty Imperials left on Dominica. Parrots also once lived on Martinique and Guadeloupe but became extinct during the eighteenth century, probably as a consequence of habitat loss and hunting. Although strong education programmes on St Lucia, St Vincent and Dominica have reduced the problem of hunting for food, the pressures to obtain birds illegally for the pet trade persist. Parrots, with their requirement for a large tract of forest to live in, are particularly vulnerable to natural catastrophes such as hurricanes. There have been some 8,000 tropical cyclones in the region in the last hundred years though most of these are of low intensity causing relatively little damage to the forests. Occasionally, however, a hurricane hits one of the islands squarely, and the damage is considerable. This happened to Dominica in 1979 with hurricane David, and again the following year after hurricane Allen swept through the region damaging also the island of St Lucia. More recently, in 1989, hurricane Hugo caused devastation to Montserrat, St Kitts-Nevis, and parts of Guadeloupe. Generally Caribbean birds are capable of withstanding such events, except when some other factor such as hunting or habitat clearance by humans has already reduced the population level to the extent that it becomes endangered with extinction.

Until rediscovered on Haiti in 1961, the black-capped petrel was presumed long extinct, although formerly occurring on the islands of Dominica, Guadeloupe and Martinique. Reasons for its extinction on these latter islands were thought to be hunting, and predation by introduced mammals such as mongoose and rats. It has recently been recorded once more on Dominica although any breeding population there must be small. Other ground-nesting seabirds have also probably suffered from human exploitation and predation by introduced animals, and most colonies are confined to inaccessible cliffs or offshore islets.

Although the problem of hunting of birds has been reduced on many of the Lesser Antillean islands by education and legislation, it continues to a large extent on the French islands of Martinique and Guadeloupe. Even on other islands, the killing of waders is a major problem, and many breeding and wintering wildfowl populations are now a fraction of their former levels. Threats to waders and waterfowl are also exacerbated by drainage of wetland areas for building or cultivation.

As increasing numbers of people discover the Caribbean, tourism itself has threatened many habitats in which birds live. This takes the form either of uncontrolled development usually along the coast, or disturbance to sensitive areas where wetland or shorebird species concentrate to feed, roost or breed. Already many coastal mangrove swamps have disappeared from St Lucia and St Vincent, and some of the extensive areas on Guadeloupe and Martinique are threatened. Some very important wetland areas exist along Salt River on St Croix, in the US Virgin Islands. This region has been proposed for development for hotel/condominium complexes, a conference centre and marinas, although an environmental education programme has been mounted to draw the attention of the public to its importance.

All of us have a responsibility to the wildlife of the Caribbean whether we make our living on the islands or visit them as tourists. We should therefore be sensitive to the pressures outlined above, each of us playing our own part in reducing those pressures by controlling our own activities and informing as many others as we can of the rich heritage they should be protecting. Those who visit the Eastern Caribbean at least partly for its scenery and wildlife are urged to write to the relevant tourist authority or government department to express those reasons for visiting the country. This will help to highlight to local governments how much priority should be given to those natural assets. Furthermore, if development unsympathetic to the natural environment is observed, it is important that it is drawn to the attention of the local government and that concerns are expressed.

Finally, we should all remember that if the forests are cleared, not only will we lose their wildlife but also there will be inevitable detrimental effects on local climate, with longer periods of drought, loss of nutrients from the soil, and ultimately poorer conditions for agriculture. If every one of us takes upon his/herself this responsibility, whether we be a farmer, politician, hotelier or tourist, the region will be a richer place for us all.

Species Accounts

GREBES   *Podicipedidae*

Pied-billed Grebe   *Podilymbus podiceps*
LENGTH: 30 – 38 cm (12 – 15 in)   LOCAL NAMES: Plongeon, Diver

This small stocky grebe is an uncommon breeding bird of shallow
freshwater, occurring mainly on the US Virgin Islands and northern
Lesser Antilles but also Guadeloupe, Martinique and Grenada.
Formerly it may have been more common but has suffered from
local hunting and loss of freshwater habitat. It is distinguished from
the **least grebe** *Tachybaptus dominicus*, the only other grebe
recorded in the region, by its much stouter, almost conical pale
beak, and in the breeding season, a black band across the bill and
black throat-patch. The upperparts are dark greyish-brown, and the
underparts mostly white. Its call is a harsh cackle breaking into
a distinctive 'kowp, kowp kowp', which slows at the end.

Grebes superficially resemble ducks but have a shorter more
compact appearance created by the very short tail, and are lobe-
footed. They rarely fly off when disturbed, preferring instead to dive
below the surface or run along the surface, with rapid, heavy wing
beats. They feed on crustaceans such as crayfish, aquatic insects
and tadpoles which they catch by propelling themselves forward
underwater with their feet. The nest is a mass of aquatic vegetation,
either floating or attached to reeds often near the water's edge, in
which up to six or seven whitish eggs are laid.

SHEARWATERS AND PETRELS   *Procellariidae*

Black-capped Petrel   *Pterodroma hasitata*
LENGTH: 33 – 40 cm (13 – 16 in)   LOCAL NAME: Diablotin

A large petrel with dark chocolate brown upperparts, a black crown
contrasting with white around the head, neck and underparts, and
a white rump. At sea it flies close to the surface, often gliding with
outstretched wings in the manner of most shearwaters. It may sit
for periods on the water, for example when feeding on its prey of
squid, flying fish and the like.

Long thought to be extinct, a large breeding colony of this
nocturnal seabird was discovered in the mountains of Haiti in

Great Shearwater

Audubon's Shearwater

1961. The species was numerous on Dominica and Guadeloupe in the early nineteenth century but then declined after human exploitation and predation by introduced animals. In Martinique it became extinct even before Europeans had settled, possibly because it was collected for food by Carib Indians. After fifty years without any definite records in the Lesser Antilles, black-capped petrels have been found again in Dominica, with individuals captured off the coast and seen flying inland; a small colony probably exists on one of the steep wooded mountains of the south-eastern coast.

Like other petrels, this species spends most of its life at sea, coming to land only during the nesting season (November – April) and then only at night. At the start of the season, its eerie, wailing cries may be heard in the vicinity of the nesting burrows, which are usually situated on remote, steep mountain slopes.

Audubon's Shearwater *Puffinus lherminieri*
LENGTH: 28 – 30 cm (11 – 12 in)

Distinguished from the previous species by the lack of a white rump and white around the nape of the neck, the Audubon's shearwater is widely distributed in tropical seas of the world. It is slightly smaller than the black-capped petrel and has a dark brown back and white underparts. Like that species, it is usually seen at sea gliding close to the surface.

It nests between November and April over a large part of the Lesser Antilles, though mainly on smaller offshore islets that are relatively inaccessible to humans. Exploitation (and perhaps also predation from rats) has been its greatest problem, nesting as it does on the ground in soil burrows, or natural cavities in sea cliffs, limestone solution holes and amongst boulders, where it lays its single white egg. On several islands, such as those east of Puerto Rico, populations have declined for this reason. One of the biggest colonies in the region was on Hardy Island, off Martinique, where 500 + pairs were breeding at least in the 1950s. Other colonies are much smaller, in most cases fifty pairs or less.

TROPICBIRDS   *Phaethontidae*

Red-billed Tropicbird   *Phaethon aethereus*
LENGTH: 90 – 106 cm (36 – 42 in) (half of which are tail streamers)

Tropicbirds are beautiful large white tern-like seabirds with long pointed wings and two very long tail streamers. In the red-billed tropicbird, the white upperparts show some narrow black barring, and there is a black eye-stripe which may extend to the nape of the neck, and a black band on the outer edge of the wing. Adults have a stout red bill but in immatures this is yellow. The two elongated central tail feathers are also absent from immatures which instead have a short pointed tail.

A widespread species of tropical oceans, red-billed tropicbirds breed in small numbers mainly in the Virgin Islands and smaller Lesser Antillean islands. The nests are usually in holes in relatively inaccessible sea cliffs with a single heavily spotted egg laid sometime between December and April. The species is often confused with the white-tailed tropicbird which appears to be the more common species in the Lesser Antilles. Although aggressive at the nest site, the species has probably suffered from human exploitation on a number of islands.

White-tailed Tropicbird in flight

Tropicbirds are most often seen near their nesting cliffs early in the morning (from dawn to around 10 a.m.), calling with a shrill scream or cackle — 'careek-careek' or 'kek-kek-kek'. At sea they feed upon flying fish and squid which they capture by plunging from a height, and then swallow either underwater or whilst floating buoyantly on the surface with tail raised into the air. They are often harried by frigatebirds which try to force them to disgorge their prey. Their flight is direct and pigeon-like with rapid strong wing beats.

White-tailed or Yellow-billed Tropicbird
Phaethon lepturus

LENGTH: 75 – 80 cm (30 – 32 in)

The white-tailed tropicbird closely resembles the previous species though slightly smaller. It is best distinguished by its white back without barring but with a heavy black band across the wing in addition to the black on the outer wing. The eye stripe is also shorter so there is no black band across the nape of the neck, and the white tail streamers are not so slender. The bill is yellow or orange. Immature red-billed and white-tailed tropicbirds could be confused since they both have yellow or orange bills and short pointed tails. However, the white-tailed tropicbird lacks the black band across the nape and is less heavily barred on the hindneck and back.

This widespread tropical species is commoner in the Eastern Caribbean than the red-billed tropicbird, and of the two, is the main one breeding on the larger Antillean islands, though always in small numbers. The single pinkish egg, heavily blotched with brown, is laid sometime between February and July (mainly March – June), in a hole in a sea-cliff. Like the previous species, it is most active close to the coast early in the morning from dawn to around 10 a.m. The cry is a harsh, shrill 'creek-creek' or 'kak-kak-kak', often repeated in a long series. Flying fish and squid form the main diet, caught by vertical plunge-dives, when the species may be molested by frigatebirds.

BOOBIES AND GANNETS
Sulidae

Brown Booby
Sula leucogaster

LENGTH: 64 – 76 cm (25 – 30 in)

The most common coastal booby in the West Indies, this species is most frequently observed flying low over the sea, alternately

White-tailed Tropicbird

Red-billed Tropicbird

Brown Booby

Red-footed Booby

flapping and gliding on long, pointed wings with head and neck outstretched. It is dark chocolate-brown in colour but with white lower breast, belly and underwing coverts. The bill is large, pointed and pale yellow in colour, often with a pinkish tinge; the feet are yellow. Immatures are entirely brown, though slightly paler below. They have a dull blackish or bluish-grey bill and dull yellowish-grey legs. The cry is a hoarse 'kak'.

Boobies usually hunt for food alone, plunge-diving to capture small fish often deep below the surface. They may also engage in aerial pursuit of flying-fish. This species is a ground nester, laying one or two white eggs either on cliff ledges or, on small low islands, on flat ground with little vegetation. The largest colonies in the region are to be found in the Virgin Islands, although these have declined considerably in the last half century. Elsewhere in the Lesser Antilles, the species nests in small numbers on Sombrero, Anguilla, Redonda, Guadeloupe, Dominica, Martinique, St Vincent and the Grenadines.

Although breeding can take place at any time of year, it usually occurs between March and July.

Red-footed Booby   *Sula sula*
LENGTH: 66 – 76 cm (26 – 30 in)

This species is white with a dark brown band on the outer wing (primaries) extending as a narrow band onto the inner wing (secondaries). The tail is white and the feet red. Immatures are dull brown but, as they grow older, most become paler on the head and underparts and have a white rump and tail, though some individuals remain in this plumage as adults. The cry is a harsh squawk or a guttural 'ga-ga-ga-ga', of variable length, often trailing away.

In the Eastern Caribbean, red-footed boobies are comparatively uncommon, possibly nesting only in the Virgin Islands (Culebra and Dutchcap Cay), on Redonda, and on St Vincent and the Grenadines. The species is colonial, each pair building an untidy nest of sticks in a bush or low tree, often in mangroves or other low vegetation. Usually only one egg is laid, sometime between March and July.

A close relative, the **masked** or **blue-faced booby** *Sula dactylatra* may be distinguished by having a much broader dark brown band on the inner wing and a dark chocolate brown (rather than white) tail. The bill and feet are variable shades of pinkish-yellow. It is the rarest of the three boobies found in the region, nesting regularly now only in the Virgin Islands (off St. Thomas, at

22

Cockroach Cay, Sula Cay and near the Tobagos). As a ground nester, it has probably been particularly vulnerable to human exploitation with substantial declines during this century.

PELICANS   *Pelecanidae*

Brown Pelican   *Pelecanus occidentalis*
LENGTH: 105 – 140 cm (41 – 55 in)

A very distinctive bird, the brown pelican is large, long-necked with an enormous throat pouch to its long grey bill. Adults have a yellowish-white head and silvery grey-brown body, the neck being mainly brown during the breeding season but all white in winter. Immatures are uniformly dull brown above and white beneath, with a brown head and neck. The head is contracted to the shoulders during flight, which is undertaken close to the water's surface by a series of strong wing-beats often followed by a short glide. It commonly soars upwards before plunge-diving vertically with wings almost folded in pursuit of fish. The species is most often seen solitarily or in small groups, flying in single file. It commonly perches on posts or exposed rocks near the water's edge.

Masked Booby   **Brown Pelican**

Although recorded virtually throughout the West Indies, the species is an uncommon visitor to most of the Lesser Antilles. Its main breeding populations occur in the US Virgin Islands but it is also reasonably common on the British Virgin Islands, Antigua, Anguilla and St Martin. Brown pelicans nest colonially near the coast or by freshwater, often in mangrove swamps. Two to four white eggs are laid in a roughly built nest usually in a bush or low tree. Pelicans breed mainly between March and July, though they can nest in any season.

Habitat loss, human disturbance and hunting have all played a part in the decline of the species over the last couple of decades. As has happened in Florida and Texas, pesticide poisoning may also be involved, for example in recent pelican deaths in Puerto Rico.

FRIGATEBIRDS   *Fregatidae*

Magnificent Frigatebird   *Fregata magnificens*
LENGTH: 95 – 110 cm (37 – 43 in)   LOCAL NAME: Frégate

The magnificent frigatebird is perhaps the seabird most frequently noticed by the casual visitor to these islands. It is often to be seen soaring with motionless arched wings high above the coast, engaged in aerial combat with another, or swooping to the surface of the sea to pick up a fish. It is a large black bird with a wingspan of up to almost 2.5 metres, a long grey hooked bill and long slender, often forked tail. The adult male has an orange or scarlet throat patch which can be inflated like a balloon during courtship. The adult female has a white breast but otherwise is also black. Immatures have a white head, breast and upper belly.

Although widely distributed throughout the region, there are few known colonies. The most important breeding site by far is in the mangrove swamps of Barbuda where between two and three thousand pairs occur; otherwise it nests in the US and British Virgin Islands (Tobago Island, Anegada, and George Dog), St Kitts and in the Grenadines. The species breeds in low trees or shrubs, building a flimsy open nest of small sticks and twigs in which the single large white egg is laid. Although usually silent in flight, at the colony they make a curious chatter or mutter with rapidly-repeated, half-guttural, half-whistling sounds that may carry several kilometres both day and night. Egg-laying occurs mainly between October and December but because of the slow growth of the young, colonies may be occupied throughout most of the year.

The diet is usually fish, taken from or near the surface by

swooping from flight and hovering. Flying-fish may be pursued in the air, whilst other seabirds are commonly chased and harassed to make them drop or disgorge their own fish prey. They never land on the water because of the difficulty they would have in taking off again.

HERONS, EGRETS and BITTERNS   *Ardeidae*

Least Bittern   *Ixobrychus exilis*
LENGTH: 28 – 35 cm (11 – 14 in)   LOCAL NAMES: Crabier, Gaulin, Bitlin

This small, secretive rusty-coloured bittern is largely ground-dwelling though sometimes to be seen perched in mangroves or other low vegetation. It is now very rare in the Eastern Caribbean where it may be found in the larger Virgin Islands, Guadeloupe and Dominica, though it may have been overlooked elsewhere.

The adult male has a glossy black crown, tail and most of the back; female and immatures have brown backs, more prominently streaked on the back (and breasts) of immatures. The hindneck and sides of the head are chestnut, though paler on the cheeks. The

Magnificent Frigatebird   **Great Blue Heron**

most distinctive features are the buff and cream patches on the upper wing. The call is a low 'coo-coo-coo-coo', the first syllable often higher than the rest, and the call slightly accelerating. There is also a loud, harsh 'cack' or series of 'tut' notes.

The species rarely flies more than a few yards when flushed from the swamp grass it favours, and more often it freezes with its bill sky-pointing. Breeding occurs from April – July, building a nest of twigs or swamp plants above standing water in which 2 – 5 pale bluish-white eggs are laid.

Great Blue Heron
LENGTH: 106 – 132 cm (42 – 52 in)

Ardea herodias
LOCAL NAME: Crabier noir

This is the largest of the dark herons, closely resembling its European counterpart, the grey heron *Ardea cinerea* except for having rufous to cinnamon thighs. Its head is largely white but with a long black plume extending back from the crown. The upperparts are mainly grey; the white underparts are streaked with black. The bill is yellow and legs yellowish-brown. Immatures are duller but with the entire crown black. The alarm call is a short series of harsh squawks, likened to the croaking of a large frog.

The great blue heron is a regular autumn and winter visitor to the Eastern Caribbean, otherwise breeding at Mangrove Lagoon, St Thomas (US Virgin Islands), Flamingo Pond Bird Sanctuary, Anegada (British Virgin Islands) and possibly also on St Croix. Resident birds are augmented by migrants and winter visitors. The species may often be seen stalking the edge of a swamp or lake in search of fish. Although primarily found near the coast in fresh or brackish water, it is sometimes seen far inland visiting small mountain lakes. A colonial breeder, the species builds its nest high in trees or amongst mangrove thickets where it lays 2 – 4 pale bluish-green eggs. The nesting season is between March and July.

Green-backed Heron
LENGTH: 40 – 48 cm (16 – 19 in)

Butorides striatus
LOCAL NAMES: Gaulin, Kio, Crabier

In the Caribbean, the green-backed heron was formerly known as the green or striated heron *Butorides virescens* but the two are now generally considered to be the same species. This small dark heron is one of the commonest in the Eastern Caribbean, occurring throughout the islands in a wide range of habitats, particularly where there is water in the form of lake, swamp or stream.

The upperparts and wings appear slate-grey tinged with green, but with buff edges to the scapulars and wing coverts. The crown is black, and in adults this may be developed into a crest. The rest of the head, neck and sides of the breast are rufous-chestnut, with a whitish stripe from the chin to the lower breast. The rest of the underparts are pale with dark streaks and spots. The bill is heavy and blackish with a yellow base to the lower mandible. The legs are shorter than other herons and egrets. They are yellow in colour but may become orange-red during the breeding season. Immatures are browner above with white spots on the upper wing, and are more heavily streaked below.

It is usually to be seen solitarily stalking the water's edge with its short neck and body arched over the surface in search of small fish, frogs or crabs. When disturbed, it utters a sharp 'kyow-kyow' or 'kyek-kyek', and flies off with strong, deep wingbeats.

Green-backed herons breed either singly or in small groups of rarely more than 5 – 6 pairs. The nest is a flimsy structure of twigs, usually built fairly low down in a tree or shrub overlooking the edge of a swamp or lake. Two to three pale blue-green eggs are laid

Green-backed Heron **Little Blue Heron**

mainly between March and July (but sometimes as late as September or October). Small numbers from North America join the resident population to winter in the Eastern Caribbean.

Little Blue Heron
LENGTH: 56 – 71 cm (22 – 28 in)

Egretta (= Florida) caerulea
LOCAL NAMES: Aigrette, Gaulin,
Pond Shakee,
Crabier Blanc – immature

A commonly observed heron in the Eastern Caribbean, the adult little blue heron is dark slate grey with a brown or chestnut head and neck. The bill is blue-grey, tipped with black and the legs are bluish-green. Immatures are strikingly different, being all-white with a dark-tipped bluish bill and greenish legs. One-year-old birds go through a transitional phase and are blotched blue and white. The call is a very throaty 'gruuh'.

Although preferring fresh or brackish water, little blue herons may be found in almost any habitat from damp pasture at sea level to montane swamp or stream at 600 – 900 m (2000 – 3000 ft). It may even be seen some distance from water, on the edge of rain forest or cultivation. The diet consists of mainly small fish, crustaceans and frogs.

The little blue heron nests in small colonies with two to four blue eggs laid sometime between February and July (sometimes to September) in a tree or shrub, usually among swamp vegetation. The species is hunted on various islands which may explain its absence since 1955 as a breeding species from Guadeloupe. A portion of the population is migratory.

A relative, the **tricolored** or **Louisiana heron** *Egretta tricolor* is a casual visitor to the Lesser Antilles, though nesting in the US Virgin Islands (Benner Bay and Mangrove Lagoon, St Thomas). It resembles the little blue heron in being dark slate-grey but with a white throat becoming rufous on the upper neck, a black bill (except for yellowish base to lower mandible), mainly black legs and yellow toes. The belly and undertail coverts are a conspicuous white. The neck is long and slender.

Cattle Egret
LENGTH: 48 – 64 cm (19 – 25 in)

Bubulcus ibis
LOCAL NAMES: Crabier, Garde Boeuf

The cattle egret is an Old World species which was virtually confined to Africa until as recently as 1930. It has since spread over large areas of the world, first occurring in the Caribbean in 1952 – 3 when individuals arrived in the Greater Antilles (Cuba and Puerto Rico). Its spread is closely associated with human pastoral activities, the species tending to occur wherever cattle are grazed. It is now the commonest heron in many islands of the region.

This small egret is all white with a yellow bill and yellow-green legs (thus distinguishing it from the snowy egret and immature little blue heron). During the breeding season, it has tufts of pinkish-buff or orange-buff feathers on the crown, lower throat and back, the bill gains an orange hue and the legs become reddish.

The species is often to be seen flocking around grazing animals such as cattle (hence its name) as they disturb the grasshoppers and other insects upon which the egrets feed. Sometimes, they will perch on the back of cattle; at other times they may stand close to their heads. They roost and nest colonially in mangrove swamps and coastal islets, laying 2 – 4 pale blue-white eggs in a nest of twigs or reeds mainly in spring and early summer. Some roosts (for example Ilet à Christophe, Guadeloupe) may number thousands of individuals, whilst a breeding colony of over 5000 birds exists in Graeme Hall Swamp, Barbados and more than one thousand nest at Fox's Bay, Montserrat.

Cattle Egret   **Common Egret**

Great or Common Egret

Casmerodius albus
(= Egretta alba)

LENGTH: 85 – 107 cm (34 – 42 in)   LOCAL NAMES: Gaulin, Grand Crabier Blanc

This is the largest white heron likely to be seen in the Eastern Caribbean. It is very distinctive, being all white with a long slender neck, yellow bill and blackish legs with a green tinge. The underside of the thigh becomes yellow in the breeding season. Adults also have beautiful long plumes on the upper breast and base of the neck, and in breeding plumage, on the shoulders (scapulars) forming a loose train. Immatures are similar to adults but lack the plumes at least until their first winter. The cry is a hoarse, throaty croak.

The common egret is actually not very common in much of the region. It breeds in the US Virgin Islands (notably St Croix but also rarely in St Thomas and St John), at Grand Cul-de-Sac Marin, Guadeloupe, and probably Baie de Fort-de-France, Martinique. However, in most of the Lesser Antilles it occurs as an uncommon though regular visitor, with birds recorded at any time of the year. Like most other herons, it favours freshwater and brackish swamps, marshes or lakes where it may be seen singly or in twos or threes standing motionless near the water's edge. Its diet is mainly fish and insects.

The species breeds colonially in trees or other swamp vegetation, building a large nest of twigs or reeds in which 2 – 5 pale blue eggs are laid. Nesting usually occurs between March and September.

Snowy Egret

Egretta thula

LENGTH: 51 – 71 cm (20 – 28 in)   LOCAL NAMES: Gaulin, Aigrette, Crabier Blanc

This most beautiful small white heron is best known for the long plumes it has hanging from its head, back and breast during the breeding season. In other plumages it can be readily distinguished from the white immature phase of the little blue heron by the presence of a black bill (with bare yellow skin at the base), black legs and bright yellow toes. Immature snowy egrets have distinctive yellowish-green backs to their legs. Flight is more buoyant than most other egrets, with a faster wingbeat. The cry is a guttural 'garr', higher pitched and more raspy than the great egret.

Snowy egrets breed in the US Virgin Islands (St Croix; rarely in St John and St Thomas), and possibly in a number of the Lesser Antilles (for example Guadeloupe and Martinique). Otherwise,

Snowy Egret   **Yellow-crowned Night Heron**

moderate numbers occur between August and March in those
islands, such as St Martin, that have reasonably large areas of
mangrove swamp. For the remaining Lesser Antillean islands, the
species is a rare though regular passage migrant or winter visitor.
The species was once the victim of the plume trade and by the
early part of this century had seriously declined in numbers.
Fortunately the sale of feathers finally became outlawed and the
species started to recover. The snowy egret is an active feeder,
darting about in shallow water after fish and crustaceans. It is a
colonial breeder, nesting low in mangrove trees or shrubs. The
species lays 2 – 5 greenish-blue eggs in a flat nest of sticks, primarily
in spring.

Yellow-crowned Night Heron   *Nycticorax (= Nyctanassa)*
violaceus

LENGTH: 55 – 71 cm (22 – 28 in)   LOCAL NAMES: Crabier, Crabier-
bois, Gaulin, Night Gaulin

This rather squat heron is mainly grey with black streaks on the
back and wings, and a distinctive black head contrasting with a
white or buff crown and white cheeks. The bill is grey-black and

31

the long legs are yellow. Immatures are grey-brown with many small light spots on the back and streaking over the rest of the body. When in flight the legs extend beyond the tail.

Although it may be seen feeding during the day, this species is most typically observed flying near coast, lake or swamp at around dusk. Its call is a short, high-pitched 'wok' or 'kwok'.

The yellow-crowned night heron is a resident in small numbers throughout the Eastern Caribbean though most common where there are extensive areas of mangrove swamp such as in the US Virgin Islands, Guadeloupe and Martinique. It breeds mainly between February and August, laying 2 – 4 pale bluish-green eggs in a platform of twigs or small branches usually in a mangrove tree or shrub, but sometimes on a cliff.

A close relative, the **black-crowned night heron** *Nycticorax nycticorax* is a casual visitor to most of the Lesser Antilles although a resident breeder in St Croix, US Virgin Islands. It is distinguished by its black crown and back, long white head plumes and white underparts. The immature is very similar but is darker and more heavily streaked with a longer more slender bill and shorter legs.

IBISES AND SPOONBILLS — *Threskiornithidae*

Glossy Ibis — *Plegadis falcinellus*

LENGTH: 55 – 64 cm (22 – 25 in)   LOCAL NAME: COCO

Although appearing all black when viewed at a distance, the glossy ibis is a very beautiful dark chestnut bird with a long thin down-curved bill and long dark olive-brown legs. Ibises fly in a distinctive manner with outstretched neck and rapid wingbeats interrupted by glides.

In the Caribbean, this swampland species breeds only in the Greater Antilles, but is a casual winter visitor to the US Virgin Islands and the more northerly Lesser Antilles. It is a colonial species, building bulky nests at moderate height in a tree and laying 3 – 4 dark blue eggs.

SWANS, GEESE AND DUCKS
Anatidae

Fulvous Whistling or Tree Duck
LENGTH: 45 – 53 cm (18 – 21 in)

Dendrocygna bicolor
LOCAL NAME: Siffleur

The fulvous whistling duck is a relatively large upright duck with a dark back and wings, a rufous-buff head and underparts, an almost black bill and blue-grey legs. It also has white markings on the flanks, a distinctive white rump and indistinct white streaks on the neck. When feeding, it spends most of the time in water, up-ending and dabbling though it can dive well.

All whistling ducks are shy and largely nocturnal, best observed flying over open swamp at dusk giving a shrill whistling call. They are relatively easy to identify in flight by their slightly hump-backed, long-necked appearance, broad wings and long legs projecting beyond the end of their short tails. Despite its alternative name, the species rarely perches in trees but walks well.

This species has a worldwide distribution. However in the Eastern Caribbean, although breeding in the swamps and lagoons of Cuba, it is no more than an irregular winter visitor to most of the Lesser Antilles (except Barbuda where it has nested recently and Antigua where it occurs throughout the year).

Fulvous Whistling Duck

Black-billed Whistling Duck

White-cheeked Pintail

Black-billed or West Indian Whistling or Tree Duck

Dendrocygna arborea

LENGTH: 48 – 58 cm (19 – 23 in)   LOCAL NAMES: Mangrove Duck, Night Duck

The only duck species confined to the West Indies, this is a dark brown bird with white on the neck and throat, blackish rump and tail, rufous breast and white belly with black spots on the flanks. The bill and legs are blackish.

With its restricted distribution, the black-billed whistling duck has been a particular casualty of the widespread hunting of wildfowl that has taken place in the Caribbean. It is now extinct in many parts of its range and declining almost everywhere. The bulk of the population occurs on the Cayman islands but small numbers also nest in Barbuda (and Puerto Rico). Elsewhere in the Eastern Caribbean, it occurs only as a vagrant.

Unlike many of the genus, this species habitually perches in trees, feeding at night on the fruits of tall Royal Palm trees. It may nest low down in tree holes, or high up among the branches of palm trees or in bromeliad clumps. The breeding season in Puerto Rico is between October and December, when 4 – 14 white eggs are laid. The species is primarily nocturnal, most often seen at dusk.

White-cheeked Pintail or Bahama Duck

Anas bahamensis

LENGTH: 38 – 51 cm (15 – 20 in)   LOCAL NAMES: Canard Tête Blanche, Summer Duck, White-head, White-throat

A small grey-brown duck with white cheeks and throat, red base to the blue-grey bill, and buffish pointed tail. The brown breast and underparts are spotted with black. The immature is similar though duller in plumage. During its fast and agile flight, the species appears slender and elegant, the brown plumage contrasting strongly with the buff rear end and white cheeks and throat. There is also a bright green speculum on the upperparts of the brown forewing bordered on either side by buff bands.

In the Eastern Caribbean, this species breeds at various sites in the US and British Virgin Islands (and Culebra and Vieques east of Puerto Rico), but is only a casual visitor to the Lesser Antilles. It occurs in coastal lagoons and mangrove swamps, shallow freshwater and brackish pools and lakes. The nesting scrape is made on dry land under a clump of vegetation, sometimes far from water, and 5 – 12 pale brown eggs are laid mainly between November and April. The species feeds by dabbling and up-ending in shallow water, although it will also feed at night among crops and stubble.

Blue-winged Teal
LENGTH: 37 – 41 cm (15 – 16 in)

Anas discors

LOCAL NAME: Sarcelle

This small brown duck species is the most common and wide-spread anatid in the Eastern Caribbean, occurring as a passage migrant or winter visitor (mainly August – April) throughout the region. In Dominica, the species has been known exceptionally to remain and breed. During the breeding season, the male develops a white facial crescent near the eye, contrasting with the dark grey head. It also has a black and white ventral region. The female is similar but with a much duller head, and a small whitish spot at the base of the bill. Both sexes have a distinctive large blue patch on the forewing which is best seen in flight.

This species may be found in brackish mangrove swamps, fresh-water marshes, lakes and ponds, feeding mainly on aquatic plants by dabbling and up-ending. They sometimes congregate into small

Blue-winged Teal

Ruddy Duck

flocks particularly at dawn or dusk. When disturbed, they fly off rapidly with an agile slightly twisting flight.

A close relative, the **green-winged teal** *Anas crecca* (which occurs throughout the northern hemisphere, and is the only teal in Europe) also occurs as an uncommon though regular winter visitor to the Eastern Caribbean. In non-breeding plumage, it is best distinguished by the absence of blue on the forewing, a larger more conspicuous green speculum (the blue-winged teal also has a green speculum but it is smaller and duller), no white facial crescent, and a smaller bill.

Other waterfowl species which occur in the Eastern Caribbean at least casually include the American wigeon *Anas americana*, northern shoveler *Anas clypeata*, lesser scaup *Aythya affinis* and ring-necked duck *Aythya collaris*.

The male **American wigeon** has a conspicuous white crown, large white patch on the forewing, and black and white abdominal region. The female is browner, with the entire head spotted black and white, and less white on the wing. It has the small blue bill tipped with black, typical of wigeons.

The **northern shoveler** is very distinctive with its broad, shovel-shaped bill. The male has a dark green head, white breast and chestnut flanks; the female is duller mottled brown, with a fleshy orange gape to the bill, and, like the male, pale sides to the tail.

The male **lesser scaup** has a small rounded glossy dark purple head, neck and breast, slightly curved blue boat-shaped bill, pale grey upperparts and white underparts, with dark rump and abdomen. The female is dull brown, darker on the wings, except for a white wing bar, with white around the base of the upper mandible, sometimes a weak whitish 'ear' patch, and a white belly.

The **ring-necked duck** resembles the lesser scaup, the male being best distinguished by its dark wings and back, the female by an indistinct white eye-ring and white at the base of the lower mandible. Both sexes have a white band across the bill and in flight lack the conspicuous white wing bar of the lesser scaup.

Ruddy Duck   *Oxyura jamaicensis*
LENGTH: 35 – 43 cm (14 – 17 in)   LOCAL NAME: Canard Plongeon

This widely distributed North and Central American duck breeds in the Eastern Caribbean now only on Grenada, where it is found primarily at Lake St Antoine. Elsewhere in the southern Lesser Antilles and US Virgin Islands, it is a casual winter visitor, having declined greatly in recent decades. The species is a small, stout duck with a stiff tail often held erect. The male is bright reddish brown with a black cap and nape, conspicuous white cheeks, and a broad blue bill. The female is mainly dark greyish brown, whitish below and a dusky streak through the whitish cheeks. It has a low, rapid whirring flight though usually it escapes disturbance by swimming and diving.

The species nests usually in waterside vegetation often on a floating platform, laying 4 – 12 large white eggs at any time of the year (but mainly between October and June). It feeds either by diving or, in shallow water, by surface dabbling.

Masked Duck
Nomonyx (= Oxyura) dominica

LENGTH: 30 – 36 cm (12 – 14 in)   LOCAL NAMES: Canard Zombie, Canard Routoutou

This small, stout duck has a broad distribution through much of Central and South America. However, in the Eastern Caribbean it nests only in Martinique and Guadeloupe, otherwise occurring as a casual winter visitor. The male has a rufous body mottled with black, a blackish face (lacking any white) and a stiff, erect tail. The female is mottled brown with whitish cheeks and two black or brown streaks one through and the other below the eye. The stout bill is blue with a black tip. Unlike the ruddy duck, it is readily flushed into the air. In flight, both sexes show a conspicuous white patch on the wings.

The species occurs on freshwater lakes and pools, building a well-hidden nest among waterside vegetation (including ricefields) and laying 8 – 18 light buff eggs mainly late in the year. It is a relatively elusive (though quite confiding) species, diving for food among water plants.

OSPREYS   *Pandionidae*

Osprey   *Pandion haliaetus*
LENGTH: 53 – 63 cm (21 – 25 in)   LOCAL NAMES: Fish Hawk,
                                    Malfini de la Mer

This large cosmopolitan hawk is a rare though regular winter visitor throughout the Eastern Caribbean. Its dark back, almost completely white head, and white underparts make it relatively easy to identify even at some distance. It is usually to be seen flying with slow, deep wingbeats along the sea-coast, near lakes or lowland rivers in search of fish. When gliding, the long wings are held in a distinctive arched position caused by a noticeable bend in each wing at the carpal joint, where there is also a black 'wrist' mark. Its call is a series of piercing mews.

The osprey captures its prey by plunge-diving and capturing fish from near the surface in its large talons. It builds a bulky nest of twigs and branches usually in a tree though it may also use man-made objects such as telegraph poles. However, although nesting attempts have been made in St Croix and Anegada, no successful breeding is known to have taken place.

Osprey

Hook-billed Kite

Chondrohierax uncinatus

LENGTH: 38 – 43 cm (15 – 17 in)   LOCAL NAME: Mountain Hawk

A robust hawk with large, deeply hooked bill, this South American species occurs in the Caribbean only on Grenada (and Trinidad). On this island it is very rare, with a population of less than 15 – 30 birds. Its distribution is mainly dry scrub woodland of south-west Grenada, determined largely by the distribution of two species of forest-dwelling snail. Except for its bill, it is rather similar to the broad-winged hawk but has underparts evenly barred brownish-yellow and white, with black barring on the undersurface of the wing. It also has a brownish-yellow collar across the nape of the neck. It feeds on tree snails, small mammals, reptiles and frogs. The bulky nest is situated high in a tree, and 2 – 3 spotted eggs are laid sometime between March and July.

Broad-winged Hawk

Buteo platypterus

LENGTH: 33 – 48 cm (13 – 19 in)   LOCAL NAMES: Malfini, Chicken Hawk

This hawk, reminiscent of the European common buzzard, has broad wings, brown upperparts and paler barred underparts, and a dark brown and white barred tail. The white underwing, breast and belly of immatures are broadly streaked with dark brown and contrast strongly with the black tips to the primaries. It is typically to be seen soaring high above the forests in the southern Lesser Antilles (Antigua, Dominica, Martinique, St Lucia, St Vincent, and Grenada) as well as occasionally Barbados. The call, a high-pitched thin squeal, gives the impression that it is made by a smaller bird.

The broad-winged hawk may sit for long periods on an exposed branch before swooping down on its prey which ranges from snakes, lizards and frogs to small birds and rodents. It nests in tall trees between March and July, laying 2 – 3 eggs in a bulky nest of twigs and branches.

Red-tailed Hawk

Buteo jamaicensis

LENGTH: 45 – 60 cm (18 – 24 in)   LOCAL NAMES: Malfini, Chicken Hawk

A larger, more stocky relative, the red-tailed hawk breeds in the Virgin Islands and Saba but occurs as a winter visitor to some of

Broad-winged Hawk in flight

Broad-winged Hawk

the northern Lesser Antilles (St Eustatius, St Kitts and Nevis; also reported from St Martin and Montserrat). It is sooty-brown above, with pale underparts contrasting with a blackish band across the belly, and in adults, a rufous tail. In the Northern Caribbean it is a common species, widespread over a range of habitats, particularly in the mountains where it may be seen soaring overhead uttering a rasping scream. It feeds on snakes, lizards, frogs, small birds and mammals. The nest is a bulky structure usually in a tall tree, and in which 2 – 3 dull white eggs are laid mainly between January and July.

Crab Hawk or Black Hawk   *Buteogallus anthracinus*
LENGTH: 50 – 58 cm (20 – 23 in)

A large, sluggish black hawk which is common in the forested mountain regions of St Vincent. It is often to be seen soaring like a *Buteo*. In flight, the black tail banded with white, dangling yellow legs, and white base of the outer wing feathers (primaries) are all useful identification features. Immatures are buffish on the underparts and undersurface of the wing, with spots or streaks of black.

41

The species is named after its habit of feeding on land crabs although it will also take crayfish and amphibians. In the Eastern Caribbean outside St Vincent, it occurs only as a vagrant to the neighbouring Grenadines and St Lucia, although it breeds in Trinidad, Cuba and parts of continental America.

FALCONS   *Falconidae*

American Kestrel or Sparrowhawk   *Falco sparverius*
LENGTH: 23 – 30 cm (9 – 12 in)   LOCAL NAMES: Gli-gli, Killy-killy, Killy Hawk

A small, agile falcon, the American kestrel is unlikely to be confused with anything except the merlin. It has a rufous back and tail, pale underparts with small black spots, and on either side of the face are two distinctive black stripes resembling side-whiskers. The male is distinguished from the female by its slate blue-grey wings.

The species often hunts from trees or telegraph poles by the roadside, dashing down to pick off lizards or large insects, which are its main prey. In flight, it has the outline typical of all falcons, with

American Kestrel   **Merlin**

long pointed wings, and a tail which narrows at the tip. Its call is a sharp 'killy-killy-killy' or 'gli-gli-gli' which gives rise to its local names.

The American kestrel is a fairly common resident of dry woodlands in the Virgin Islands and northern Lesser Antilles, though absent or only a casual visitor south of St Lucia. It nests in a tree cavity or base of a palm, laying 2 – 5 eggs speckled with reddish brown. Breeding takes place between February and July.

Merlin or Pigeon Hawk *Falco columbarius*
LENGTH: 25 – 34 cm (10 – 13 in)   LOCAL NAME: Gri-gri de Montagne

The merlin is a regular passage migrant and winter visitor to the Eastern Caribbean, occurring in most months of the year (but mainly between October and March) in the Virgin Islands and most of the northern Lesser Antilles. Further south it appears to be only a casual visitor. It resembles a small version of the peregrine, the male being slate-grey above, with pale or buffish underparts streaked with black and the relatively long tail barred with black. The female has dark brown upperparts rather than rufous as in the American kestrel with which it might otherwise be confused.

During migration, the species occurs in any habitat from sea level to mountain top. It feeds on small birds, lizards and large insects which are picked off by direct low flight with steady wingbeats.

Peregrine Falcon *Falco peregrinus*
LENGTH: 38 – 55 cm (15 – 22 in)

This largest of falcons occurring in the Eastern Caribbean, has a black moustachial stripe contrasting with the white chin and cheeks, slate-grey upperparts (brown in immatures), and a barred tail. The underparts are buffish or white, streaked and spotted with black. In flight it has a distinctive anchor-like outline of long pointed wings and relatively short narrow tail, with fast shallow wing-beats followed by a glide. It is perhaps best known for its powerful and rapid, steep dives with almost closed wings in pursuit of other birds upon which it feeds. The call, a harsh chattering 'kek-kek-kek-kek', is mainly uttered near the nest site.

In many parts of the world this species has suffered through the use of pesticides such as DDT. These persistent chemicals sprayed over farmland are ingested by small birds which in turn are taken by peregrines. The concentrations build up along the food chain, reaching levels that caused eggshell thinning and breeding failure

Peregrine Falcon

in peregrine populations. Only now, where there have been reductions in the use of these pesticides, the species is making a comeback. It is a regular, though rare, winter visitor from North America, occurring throughout the Eastern Caribbean, although resident and recently recorded breeding on Dominica. It is found mainly along the coast, over cliffs or mangrove swamps, although it may visit any habitat including rain forest and cultivation.

CURASSOWS, GUANS AND CHACHALACAS   *Cracidae*

Rufous-vented Chachalaca   *Ortalis ruficauda*
LENGTH: 58 cm (22 in)   LOCAL NAME: Cocrico

A turkey-like bird which occurs in northern Bequia and western Union in the Grenadines, where it was probably brought from Tobago or Venezuela although it has been in the islands since at least the late seventeenth century. The upperparts are olive brown but with a grey head and hindneck. The tail is very long and broad with an iridescent sheen, the outer feathers broadly tipped with chestnut. The underparts are a drab grey, blackish on the centre of the throat and rufous on the flanks and undertail coverts. There is dark-blue bare skin around the eye and red bare sides to the throat.

This ground-dwelling species feeds mainly on berries, small fruits and young shoots. It normally remains in thick shrubbery, trees or coconut palms. Its call is a very loud, raucous 'cocrico', repeated several times. It also makes a subdued chuckling sound when feeding. The relatively small nest is built in a bush or tree a short distance above the ground, into which usually three white eggs are laid.

RAILS, GALLINULES AND COOTS   *Rallidae*

Clapper Rail   *Rallus longirostris*
LENGTH: 30 – 38 cm (12 – 15 in)   LOCAL NAMES: Pond Shakee, Pintade

This large rail is greyish-brown with a short neck and long slightly downturned bill. The throat is whitish becoming greyish or buff on the breast then barred black and white on the belly and abdomen. Rarely seen, its call is a loud, grating series of 'keks' slowing at the end.

The clapper rail is resident in or around mangrove swamps of the Greater Antilles including the US Virgin Islands, and the northern Lesser Antilles (Antigua and Guadeloupe). It nests usually among mangrove roots, laying 5 – 9 whitish or buff, spotted eggs at any time of year but mainly between April and June or October and November. Rails are very shy and more easily heard than seen, the call being a series of harsh ticks. They tend to run off when disturbed, and they feed upon crabs, snails, insects and vegetable matter.

Sora, Sora Rail or Sora Crake   *Porzana carolina*
LENGTH: 18 – 23 cm (7 – 9 in)   LOCAL NAME: Rale

This distinctive small rail has a very short chicken-like yellow bill. The upperparts are olive-brown mottled with black narrowly streaked with white. In the adult, the front of the face, chin and upper breast are black (less pronounced in females and absent in immatures). The remainder of the breast is grey becoming white on the abdomen, and the flanks barred black and white. The feet are green.

The sora occurs as a winter visitor in freshwater swamps (also mangroves) with thick vegetation throughout the Eastern Caribbean. It is more readily flushed than other rails, making short, though weak flights. Its call is a whistled 'ker-wee' or a musical descending 'whinny'.

Common Moorhen or Gallinule
LENGTH: 28 – 33 cm (11 – 13 in)

Gallinula chloropus

LOCAL NAMES: Poule d'eau à Cachet Rouge, Red-seal Coot

This brown-backed, otherwise sooty black waterbird has a red frontal shield extending to the base of its short bill. The tip of the bill is yellow-green and the legs green with red above the knees. A white band exists along the flanks with white under the tail. It swims making jerking movements of the head, and is relatively noisy with harsh hen-like clucks or squawks, including a piercing laugh-like cackle slowing at the end, 'ki-ku-ki-ki-ka, kaa, kaaa'.

This species is a common resident of swamps, lakes and pools throughout the Eastern Caribbean. It feeds on aquatic plants, snails and other aquatic invertebrates, swimming mainly along the edge of open water. When disturbed, it runs over the surface with wings flapping in its attempt to seek cover in dense vegetation. The nest is usually amongst reeds near the surface, where 3 – 9 spotted eggs are laid mainly between September and March (but can be any time of year).

A relative, the **purple gallinule** *Porphyrula martinica*, is distinguished by its green back, blue or purple head and underparts and white forehead. The uniformly brown immature is best distinguished from a young common gallinule by the lack of a white side stripe. The purple gallinule is at most a very rare winter visitor to the US Virgin Islands (St John and St Thomas; formerly St Croix), and Lesser Antilles, though breeding has been reported from Guadeloupe.

Caribbean Coot
LENGTH: 38 – 40 cm (15 – 16 in)

Fulica caribaea

LOCAL NAMES: Poule d'Eau à Cachet Blanc, White-seal Coot.

This sooty-grey bird with a black neck and head is reminiscent in shape of the gallinule but has a conspicuous broad white shield on the forehead and a white bill tipped with black. Also the head is larger and the neck shorter than the gallinule. Otherwise, like gallinules, it swims buoyantly with nodding head, and runs on the water to take off. Its call is a variety of clucks or cackling sounds.

It is an uncommon resident breeding in the US and British Virgin Islands, St Martin/Maarten, Montserrat, Guadeloupe, Martinique and Grenada, having declined greatly in numbers due to loss of habitat and over-hunting. The species is usually found on the edge of open water of lakes, ponds or swampy areas. It will feed at and

Common Moorhen   **Purple Gallinule**

Caribbean Coot

below the surface on aquatic plants, insects and small fish, as well as upon land on seeds or roots. It builds a nest amongst aquatic vegetation, laying 4 – 8 speckled white eggs at any time of year but mainly between December and February.

The **American coot** *Fulica americana* is a close relative, possibly one and the same species, best distinguished by a small red rather than white frontal shield behind its white bill. It is a winter visitor in small numbers from North America to the Greater Antilles, though uncommon in the Virgin Islands, and is rare in the Lesser Antilles (Antigua, Guadeloupe, Martinique and Barbados). In some areas (for example Mary Point Pond, St John) the American coot is resident, and the two species may hybridise with one another.

PLOVERS AND TURNSTONES *Charadriidae*

Lesser or American Golden-Plover *Pluvialis dominica*
LENGTH: 24 – 28 cm (9 – 11 in)

This species so named because of its gold-spangled upperparts in breeding plumage, is a regular passage migrant in small numbers throughout the Eastern Caribbean, particularly on open fields or golf courses. It occurs in the region mainly between August and November, with a few also between February and April.

Birds in non-breeding plumage are grey-brown above (sometimes with vestiges of gold), and have a grey breast and whitish belly. Males in breeding plumage have a striking black face and cheeks, breast stripe and belly with large white patches on the flanks extending behind the cheeks. The back is grey flecked with gold. The bill is short and fairly thick and the fairly long legs are black. In all plumages, the species has a distinct white eye stripe which may be a useful identification feature in flight. The call is a rapid 'tu-ee' or 'chu-wit', and a plaintive 'kl-ee' or 'ki-wee'.

The similar **black-bellied** or **grey plover** *Pluvialis squatarola* is much paler with grey upperparts spotted with white, a distinct dark patch behind the eye, and no obvious white eye-stripe. It is larger and plumper in outline and has a black face and belly only when in breeding plumage. The species may also be distinguished in flight by a strong white wing bar and squarish white patch on the rump and uppertail. From underneath, the black 'armpits' are very obvious in flight. Black-bellied plovers migrate mainly in July – November and February – May through the Caribbean. However, in St Martin/Maarten, largest numbers are seen in December and

Lesser Golden-Plover   **Black-bellied Plover**

January, although the species is mainly seen in the Greater Antilles. During migration, they can occur not only on beaches but also inland beside pools or on pastures. The call is a very distinctive, loud slurred whistle, 'tlee-oo-ee', the second syllable lower in pitch. It also makes a single, plaintive 'klee'.

Wilson's or Thick-billed Plover   *Charadrius wilsonia*
LENGTH: 18 – 20 cm (7 – 8 in)   LOCAL NAMES: Sand Bird, Little Ploward, Nit, Thick-billed Plover

The Wilson's plover resembles the semi-palmated plover but has a thick black bill and grey legs sometimes tinged with pink. It is grey-brown above, with a white forehead extending behind the eye, a white collar, and a broad black (breeding male) or brown (female and non-breeders) band across the chest. Immatures have darker brown upperparts with buff fringes. The call is a high, weak, whistled 'whit' or 'wheet', or a quick 2 – 3 syllable 'ki-ki-ki'.

The species is a common resident breeder on coastal beaches, sand and sometimes mud flats in the Greater Antilles (including the US Virgin Islands), occurring regularly also in the northern Lesser Antilles south to Antigua. Further south it is virtually

49

absent. Two to four spotted, light buff-coloured eggs are laid directly on the sand in a shallow scrape, mainly in spring. Its diet is primarily crabs.

Semipalmated Plover   *Charadrius semipalmatus*
LENGTH: 17 – 19 cm (7 – 8 in)

This species, the American counterpart of the European ringed plover *Charadrius hiaticula*, is small, with a short stubby black bill (orange-yellow at the base in non-breeding birds) and yellow or orange legs. There is a narrow black or grey breast band, the upperparts are grey-brown and the underparts white. In flight it shows a long white wingbar and the call is a clear, fairly sharp, rising whistle, 'chuwit' or 'chu-wee', or a plaintive 'weet'.

Breeding in Arctic North America, the species migrates through the Caribbean, mainly between August and November, although non-breeding birds may be seen in any month of the year. It is common in the Greater Antilles including the US Virgin Islands, but occurs in small numbers throughout the Lesser Antilles.

Semipalmated Plover   **American Oystercatcher**

A relative, the **killdeer** *Charadrius vociferus*, is distinguished by its larger size, longer tail, and two black breast bands. It is a resident breeder in the Greater Antilles (including the US Virgin Islands), also commonly recorded in St Martin/Maarten but a rare transient migrant or winter visitor to the remaining Lesser Antilles. Likewise, the **snowy** or **Kentish plover** *Charadrius alexandrinus*, breeds in the Greater Antilles (for example Cabo Rajo Salt Flats in Puerto Rico; also Anegada). It has been found breeding on St Maarten and until recently it was breeding in St Croix but now occurs only as a non-breeder in the Virgin Islands and a very casual, mainly summer visitor elsewhere in the Lesser Antilles. The **collared plover** *Charadrius collaris*, breeds in Central America and Trinidad, but may also do so in Grenada, Mustique (Grenadines) and Barbados where it has been recorded.

OYSTERCATCHERS   *Haematopodidae*

American Oystercatcher   *Haematopus palliatus*
LENGTH: 44 – 48 cm (17 – 19 in)   LOCAL NAME: Caracolero,
                                              Whelkcatcher

The oystercatcher is a cosmopolitan shorebird which breeds in a number of the Greater Antilles including St Thomas in the US Virgin Islands. It is a regular non-breeding bird occurring throughout the year on the cays of the British Virgin Islands, but is generally absent from the Lesser Antilles except St Martin/Maarten where it may breed. The species is very distinctive with a black head and neck, greyish-brown back, wings and tail, except for a large white patch on the wings and white on the uppertail coverts. The breast and belly are also white. The long bill is bright orange-red, the eyelids red and the feet are pale pink. This bird is most often seen along the coast, flying swiftly past with a loud repeated, 'wheep-wheep-wheep'. It feeds on mussels and other molluscs by probing them open with its bill. A scrape is made in sand or gravel, sometimes bare rock, where 1 – 3 spotted buff-coloured eggs are laid, mainly in May – June.

AVOCETS AND STILTS · *Recurvirostridae*

Black-necked or Black-winged Stilt
Himantopus mexicanus

LENGTH: 35 – 40 cm (13 – 15 in)   LOCAL NAMES: Redshank, Soldier, Crackpot Soldier, Telltale, Pète-pète

This elegant-looking wader has a black crown, hindneck and back contrasting with white above the eye, a white forehead and underparts, a long slender slightly upturned black bill, and very long pinkish-red legs. The female has a browner mantle than the male.

It is a resident of coastal lagoons and brackish ponds, commonest from March – October, breeding in the Greater Antilles including the US and British Virgin Islands, and in the northern Lesser Antilles (for example Antigua and St Martin/Maarten). However, from Guadeloupe southwards, it occurs only as a casual autumn or winter visitor. It feeds actively in shallow water on aquatic insects. It is comparatively noisy, making a sharp barking sound, 'kek', which may be uttered in rapid succession. The nest is a platform of grass and twigs in which 3 – 7 blotched, olive-green eggs are laid mainly between late April and August.

WOODCOCK, SNIPE AND SANDPIPERS · *Scolopacidae*

These form a large family of wading birds, with most representatives only visiting the Caribbean on migration from their arctic breeding grounds. Several species may be seen in the Eastern Caribbean particularly between August and November. Those considered below represent only the more common ones or those that actually breed in the region. Bird-watchers are recommended to use one of the North American bird handbooks when wader-watching in the Caribbean at this time, and to be prepared for sightings of species not described here.

Spotted Sandpiper
Actitis macularia

LENGTH: 18 – 20 cm (7 – 8 in)   LOCAL NAME: Weather Bird

This is one of the most commonly observed small sandpipers in the Eastern Caribbean. It breeds throughout most of North America, migrating south to spend the winter. However, non-breeding individuals may be seen in the Greater and Lesser Antilles at any time of year.

Spotted Sandpiper

It is distinctive by its bobbing walk, and flickering flight with short shallow wing beats. The upperparts are olive brown, the underparts white extending upward to the shoulder in front of the wing. The black spotting on the underparts from which its name derives, occurs only in breeding plumage. The legs are yellowish and the bill has a contrasting pale base and dark tip. The tail is short, extending only a short distance beyond the wings.

The spotted sandpiper is usually seen in the vicinity of water, along coasts or near lagoons, ponds or rivers. It is solitary in habit, and when disturbed utters a series of shrill, faintly rising 'peet' notes. The species is the American counterpart of the common sandpiper *Actitis hypoleucos* of Eurasia.

One sandpiper which could be confused with this species is the **solitary sandpiper** *Tringa solitaria*. This is a regular passage migrant (particularly between August and October) and occasional winter resident throughout the Eastern Caribbean. It is best distinguished by its larger, more slender form with darker legs and much greater contrast between the white belly and its much darker upperparts. Its long, pointed dark wings and swift, erratic flight distinguish it on the wing. When alarmed, it utters a hard, emphatic series of whistles, 'weet-weet-weet'. This species is the American counterpart of the Eurasian green sandpiper *Tringa ochropus*.

Solitary Sandpiper Turnstone

Lesser Yellowlegs

Turnstone or Ruddy Turnstone   *Arenaria interpres*
LENGTH: 21 – 25 cm (8 – 10 in)

A short-legged chunky shorebird, the ruddy turnstone, though usually seen in the Eastern Caribbean on autumn or spring migration, may be found at any time of year. In non-breeding plumage it has a mainly dark brown head with buffish-white chin, mostly dark grey-brown breast surrounding irregular whitish patches on the side of the throat, and a white belly. The bill is small, slender and black, and the legs orange. In flight, it appears strikingly patterned with dark and white on the upper wings and white on the underwings and rest of the underparts. The call is a rapid staccato 'trik-tuk-tuk' or shorter 'tuk-e-tuk'.

In breeding plumage, the species acquires striking chestnut upperparts with black across the wing coverts, sharply patterned black and white on the head and breast, the remainder of the belly and undertail being conspicuously white.

The ruddy turnstone is most often seen near the coast along sandy beaches, mudflats and pond edges, where it scavenges for small crustaceans and insects. Its flight is strong and direct, usually low with rather stiff and shallow wingbeats.

Lesser Yellowlegs   *Tringa flavipes*
LENGTH: 23 – 25 cm (9 – 10 in)

This is the commonest of the larger shorebirds in the Eastern Caribbean, occurring throughout the region as a passage migrant and winter visitor. It may in fact be seen in any month of the year though particularly between July and November. Like most of the sandpipers, it breeds in northern North America.

It is a tall elegant wader with a straight slim black bill and long bright orange-yellow legs. The upperparts and upper breast are grey or brownish-grey with whitish or buff spots, and the belly is white. In flight, it shows a neat square patch of white on the rump, contrasting with the dark tail, back and upperwings. The feet project beyond the tail tip.

The lesser yellowlegs occurs mainly on the edge of brackish and freshwater ponds and lagoons, but also on damp meadows and pasture. It is commonly seen in company with sandpipers and other waders. Its call is a rather nasal, whistled 'tew-tew'.

Greater Yellowlegs
Tringa melanoleuca
LENGTH: 29 – 33 cm (12 – 13 in)

Almost identical to the previous species, the greater yellowlegs is best distinguished by its larger size and heavier build, and longer slightly upturned bill (1.5 × the head length compared with just over 1 × head length in lesser yellowlegs). It is also very similar in flight though larger and more powerful with clear white notches on the inner wing (secondaries). The call is more distinct, being a louder, ringing, clear 'teu-teu-teu' on a slightly descending scale.

The greater yellowlegs is a regular passage migrant (particularly autumn) and winter visitor throughout the Eastern Caribbean, though in smaller numbers than the lesser yellowlegs. It occurs in similar habitat to its smaller relative and the two may often be seen together.

Another species, the **willet** *Catoptrophorus semipalmatus*, resembles the greater yellowlegs but has paler brownish-grey or grey upperparts, giving less contrast with the white underparts. It also has a larger heavier bill and thick, dark blue-grey legs. In flight, it shows conspicuous long white wingbars crossing the entire wing. It is so named for its musical 'pill-will-willet' call. It also makes a sharp 'chip-chip-chip'. The willet breeds on St Croix and Anegada, where it nests on beaches, laying a clutch of four spotted eggs in a scrape. It may also breed in the northern Lesser Antilles on Antigua and St Martin/Maarten but is a rare migrant on other Virgin Islands and elsewhere in the Lesser Antilles, occurring as a casual visitor mainly between August and November.

Pectoral Sandpiper
Calidris melanotos
LENGTH: 19 – 24 cm (9 – 10 in)

This sandpiper, with its fairly short, faintly down-curved bill and shortish, usually yellowish legs, resembles the least sandpiper but is larger and has a distinct dark streak on the breast which sharply contrasts with the white belly. In flight, the wings look dark with only a very faint white wing bar. The typical flight call is a loud, harsh, reedy 'churk' or 'trrit', often irregularly repeated.

The species is a fairly common passage migrant (mainly between July and November) throughout the Eastern Caribbean. Like the next two species, with which it may be seen, the pectoral sandpiper occurs along lagoons, the edges of swamps, lakes, and wet meadows, often feeding amongst vegetation away from the water's edge.

Willet

Greater Yellowlegs

Pectoral Sandpiper

Semipalmated Sandpiper *Calidris pusilla*
LENGTH: 13 – 15 cm (5 – 6 in)

This small sandpiper is probably the most abundant of all shore-birds in the Eastern Caribbean, occurring throughout the region as a passage migrant particularly between July and November. Small numbers of non-breeders may be found throughout the year, whilst in suitable areas, on passage, flocks may comprise up to a few thousand birds.

The species has rather plain grey-brown upperparts, the sides of the breast washed with grey and faintly streaked, white underparts, a short black bill and black legs. The bill is blunt tipped and rather deep at the base. The back feathers become buff-tipped, even rufous, only in breeding plumage, giving a scaly appearance. In flight, it shows a narrow white wing bar and white sides to the rump and uppertail. The flight call is a hoarse, shrill 'cherk' or 'chrup', sometimes with a soft chittering call on take off.

On migration the semipalmated sandpiper occurs along lagoons and mudflats, the edges of swamp and lake, beaches and damp pasture. The species feeds by intermittent probing of the mud for tiny semi-aquatic organisms.

It is very similar to the slightly larger **western sandpiper** *Calidris mauri*, a much rarer passage migrant and winter visitor (mainly

Semipalmated Sandpiper

Western Sandpiper

58

September – March) to the region. The latter is best distinguished by its finer-tipped and slightly down-turned bill, and its thin but sharp, querulous 'jeet' call. It feeds in slightly deeper water along mudflats and on the edges of pools.

Least Sandpiper   *Calidris minutilla*
LENGTH: 13 – 16 cm (5 – 6½ in)

The least sandpiper is the smallest wader in the world. It resembles the semipalmated sandpiper but has yellow or greenish legs and much browner, darker upperparts. It also has a typical almost crouching posture and the blackish bill appears more slender with a pointed slightly drooping tip. In flight it looks very similar to that species but its call is a high-pitched, shrill, rising 'trreee', often given in a slow irregular series, a lower 'prrrt', and a thin, soft whistle 'wi-wi-wit'.

Though less common than the semipalmated sandpiper, the least sandpiper is nevertheless a regular passage migrant and winter visitor (mainly August – May) throughout the Eastern Caribbean, and often occurs alongside that species. It frequents coastal lagoons and swamp and lake edges, and damp pasture, less commonly occurring along beaches.

Least Sandpiper

Short-billed Dowitcher   *Limnodromus griseus*
LENGTH: 26 – 30 cm (10 – 12 in)

This wader, of snipe-like appearance, has a long, straight bill, greenish legs, grey upperparts and breast, the latter streaked and speckled on the lowerparts, merging to a white belly. In flight, a long oval white patch shows on the back, and there is also white on the trailing edge of the wings. The flight call is a rapid mellow 'tu-tu-tu', faster than the similar call of the lesser yellowlegs.

The species is a regular passage migrant and winter visitor (mainly August – April) in small numbers throughout the Eastern Caribbean, occurring around lagoons, mud flats, lake edges and damp pastures. It usually feeds in water, often submerging the head with rapid snipe-like vertical probing. Those birds occurring in the Caribbean are from populations that breed in eastern arctic Canada.

Visitors to the Eastern Caribbean should look out for the closely related **long-billed dowitcher** *Limnodromus scolopaceus*. Only recently recognised as a distinct species, it is best distinguished by its longer bill and distinctive high, thin 'keek' call. The tail also always has large dark bars across it. In breeding plumage, the underparts are a deeper red to the lower belly, with barred flanks, compared with the paler rufous underparts and spotted flanks of the short-billed dowitcher. Although in the Eastern Caribbean, the long-billed dowitcher has been recorded so far only definitely from the Virgin Islands, it is likely that it occurs elsewhere as a rare passage migrant and winter visitor.

Stilt Sandpiper   *Calidris (= Micropalama) himantopus*
LENGTH: 18 – 23 cm (7 – 9 in)

This species bears a superficial resemblance to the short-billed dowitcher, feeding in water with rapid, irregular vertical probing of the bill. However, it is much smaller, with a shorter bill, slightly slimmer neck and longer legs. Its upperparts are brown-grey and underparts white but with clear grey streaking on the lower neck and breast. In flight, a square white patch shows up distinctly on the rump, as in the lesser and greater yellowlegs, but it is much smaller with legs projecting further beyond the tail. The flight call is usually a soft rattling trill 'kirrr' or 'grrrt', or a clearer 'whu'.

The stilt sandpiper is a fairly common passage migrant, mainly between July and November, to the Eastern Caribbean. It is most often found around lagoons and lake edges rather than along open shores.

Short-billed Dowitcher

Stilt Sandpiper

GULLS AND TERNS

Laridae

Laughing Gull

Larus atricilla

LENGTH: 40 – 45 cm (16 – 18 in)   LOCAL NAMES: Sea Gull, Booby, Gullie

This, the only gull species nesting in the Caribbean, breeds throughout the region though usually in scattered small colonies. The main breeding concentration occurs on the islands east of Puerto Rico to Anegada. Although rarer in winter, some non-breeding individuals may be seen at any time of year throughout the region.

This gull has a dark sooty-grey head in breeding plumage, but in winter this becomes white mottled with grey on the top and sides. The rest of the upperparts are grey with black wing-tips, and the underparts are white. Immatures have a brown head, wings and back. The call is 'ha-ha-ha-ha', hence its name!

The laughing gull feeds from the sea surface or along the shore on fish and offal. It may also be seen feeding inland on pasture. It nests on the ground in a shallow depression, laying 2 – 4 greenish, spotted eggs mainly between April and July.

Four other gull species, though still vagrant, are being recorded in the region with increasing frequency. They are the **ring-billed gull** *Larus delawarensis*, **herring gull** *L. argentatus*, **great black-backed** *L. marinus* and **lesser black-backed** *L. fuscus* gulls. In adult plumage each is distinctive, but immatures can be confused. Young herring gulls in their first winter have a dark head and tail; great black-backed and lesser black-backed gulls have a whiter head, rump, tail and underparts, the great black-backed having the most white on the head and over the nape of the neck. The ring-billed gull is much smaller than the black-backed gull, and rather smaller than the herring gull, with a black band across the bill, a pale grey mantle, and narrow black terminal band across the end of the tail.

Laughing Gull   **Royal Tern**

Royal Tern

LENGTH: 45 – 50 cm (18 – 20 in)

Sterna maxima

LOCAL NAMES: Sprat Bird, Gullie, Egg Bird, Gaby

The royal tern may be seen at any time of year throughout the Eastern Caribbean. However, most breeding colonies are small and occur primarily on the islands just east of Puerto Rico and Flat Key, St Thomas (Virgin Islands).

The species is a large crested tern with a heavy orange or yellow bill and relatively slow wingbeat. The feet are black and the tail moderately forked. Its call is a shrill 'kri-k-ik', 'kee-rer' or 'kirrup', and also a bleating 'ee-ah'.

It is mainly seen near the sea-shore, feeding almost entirely on fish. It usually nests in colonies on small cays, with one, occasionally two, spotted white or pale buff-coloured eggs laid mainly between April and July.

Four other smaller white terns breed in the Eastern Caribbean. The **sandwich tern** *Sterna sandvicensis* (with black bill tipped with yellow) nests on Culebra (east of Puerto Rico), Sombrero and the Virgin Islands (mainly Anegada and Pelican Cay off St Thomas where it sometimes breeds with the very similar all yellow-billed **cayenne tern** *Sterna eurygnatha*), but in the Lesser Antilles only in Guadeloupe.

The **roseate tern** *Sterna dougallii* (with mainly black bill, but with red on the basal half) breeds in moderate numbers on the same Greater Antillean islands, with small scattered colonies in the Lesser Antilles. The **common tern** *Sterna hirundo* (also with a mainly black bill with red at the base) does not appear to breed regularly in the region except in the Virgin Islands (Little Flat Cay, Saba Cay, Dog Island, Shark Island); elsewhere, it occurs as an uncommon migrant mainly between August and October. Confusion between common and roseate terns has often occurred in the past since the latter species in the Caribbean has more red on the bill than elsewhere. They are best distinguished by the much paler upperparts, longer more deeply-forked tail, longer deeper bill, and distinctive call (a soft 'chew-ick' and infrequent rasping 'aach') of the roseate tern. The common tern also has much darker panels on the forewing.

The fourth breeding white tern is the **least tern** *Sterna antillarum* (much smaller, with yellow, black-tipped bill, and yellow legs). This species nests in relatively small colonies on the Virgin Islands and offshore islands east of Puerto Rico and along the coast of St Martin/Maarten, but is a rare breeder elsewhere in the Lesser Antilles. It is considered by many authorities to be conspecific with the Eurasian little tern *Sterna albifrons*.

Bridled Tern   *Sterna anaethetus*
LENGTH: 35 – 38 cm (14 – 15 in)   LOCAL NAMES: Egg Bird, Booby

This is a widespread and common breeder throughout the Eastern Caribbean, with concentrations totalling around 2000 pairs on the Virgin Islands, Culebra and Cordillera (just east of Puerto Rico). In the Lesser Antilles, colonies are all small, rarely numbering more than 100 pairs.

The bridled tern has a brownish-grey back, wings and tail, a black crown with conspicuous white forehead extending back above and behind the eye, white on the hindneck and white underparts. The bill and legs are dark. Immatures have a white head and hindneck, with the crown streaked with black, the rest of the back being dark brown. Its call is distinctive, a high-pitched, querulous 'wep-wep' or 'wup-wup'.

The species nests on relatively inaccessible cliffs or remote islets, often concealed under low vegetation, amongst boulders or

Roseate Tern　　　　　　　　　**Bridled Tern**

in cliff-holes. One or two whitish eggs are laid in a shallow scrape mainly between April and July. It spends most of its life far off shore, feeding primarily upon fish, but will also take planktonic crustaceans and molluscs.

Sooty Tern　　　　　　　　　　　*Sterna fuscata*
LENGTH: 38 – 43 cm (15 – 17 in)　　LOCAL NAMES: Egg Bird, Booby, Hurricane Bird

By far the most numerous breeding seabird in the Caribbean, the sooty tern nests throughout the region. Largest numbers (between 100 000 and 200 000 pairs) nest on the Virgin Islands, Culebra and Cordillera (east of Puerto Rico). In the Lesser Antilles, colonies are generally much smaller, although between 10 000 and 20 000 pairs nest on Aves Island, west of Dominica and about 50 000 were recorded in a breeding colony on Ilet Poirier, near Baie des Anglais, Martinique.

The species is very similar to the bridled tern with which it has often been confused in the past. It is best distinguished by its darker, almost black back and wings, so that the black crown

65

Sooty Tern

Brown Noddy

merges with the nape of the neck, and by the smaller white patch on the forehead (extending no further than the eye). It also has a longer, more deeply forked tail though this is not a very good identification feature. Immatures have sooty brown upperparts spotted with white, the underparts being paler and greyer. The call is a nasal 'ker-wacky-wack' and a rasping 'krek'.

Sooty terns nest on sea-cliffs and remote islets, laying one, occasionally two, spotted eggs mainly between April and July, although in the larger colonies, breeding may take place somewhat earlier during December to February. The nest is merely a depression in a cliff hole, amongst boulders or in thick vegetation (for example cactus plants). Like the previous species, it spends most of its life at sea, feeding mainly upon fish which it takes from the surface. A major problem facing this species, as with other seabirds, is large-scale egg-collecting. This continues at many sites including the British Virgin Islands and Aves Island. The eggs are locally referred to as 'booby' eggs and are considered to be aphrodisiacs. The huge colony on Punta Flamenco, Culebra has been greatly reduced, possibly by habitat changes due to grazing.

Brown Noddy

LENGTH: 37 – 38 cm (15 in)

Anous stolidus

LOCAL NAMES: Egg Bird, Booby, Blackbird

The brown noddy is the second most numerous seabird nesting throughout the Eastern Caribbean. The main concentrations occur in the Virgin Islands where somewhere between 2000 and 4000 pairs breed, although fairly large numbers breed on islets off the east coast of Antigua.

It is much darker than other terns, being sooty brown all over except for a very pale grey or white forehead and crown. The tail is wedge-shaped. Immatures are whitish on the forehead only. Its call is a low-pitched 'kark' and a scolding 'kwok, kwok'.

The species nests in a variety of habitats, ranging from trees and shrubs in mangroves, to flat, sparsely vegetated ground as well as on bare rock on cliff ledges. The single, slightly spotted buffish egg is laid mainly between April and July, either in a shallow depression or in a rough nest of twigs. Outside the breeding season, the species spends most of its time off shore. It feeds on small fish taken at the surface.

PIGEONS AND DOVES

Columbidae

White-crowned Pigeon

Columba leucocephala

LENGTH: 33 – 36 cm (13 – 14 in)

LOCAL NAMES: Ramier, Tête-blanche, Blue Pigeon, White Head, Baldpate

This large, dark, slate-grey pigeon has a conspicuous white crown and an iridescent nape to the neck. The bill is red with a white tip. Females have a less distinct greyish white crown whilst in immatures it is smoky grey. Its call is a very low-pitched 'crooo-cru, coo-cooo, crooo' or repeated 'coo-croo', similar to the cooing of the European Wood Pigeon, with a rising second syllable.

The white-crowned pigeon is an uncommon breeding resident in the Greater Antilles. Although occurring locally in midlevel and lowland woodlands, fields and around towns in Puerto Rico, in the Virgin Islands it remains fairly common only in some mangroves on the smaller, undisturbed islands. Numbers are augmented in autumn and winter by migrants from elsewhere. It also breeds in small numbers in the northern Lesser Antilles but, south of Guadeloupe, is no more than a casual visitor. The species may once have occurred throughout the region, there being old records from some other Antillean islands. However, in many areas it has been hunted to near extinction.

The species roosts and nests in colonies, in trees, shrubs or cactus plants, commonly on cays or in mangrove swamps. The flimsy nest is built of twigs and grasses and 1 – 2 white eggs are laid mainly between March and July (sometimes to September). It feeds on the fruits and seeds of a variety of trees and may also take cultivated grain.

Scaly-naped or Red-necked Pigeon

Columba squamosa

LENGTH: 36 – 40 cm (14 – 16 in)

LOCAL NAMES: Ramier, Ramier Cou-rouge, Blue Pigeon, Mountain Pigeon

The red-necked or scaly-naped pigeon is also a dark slate-grey bird but it differs strikingly from the previous species in its head markings. It has a dull reddish-purple head, front of the neck and chest, with chestnut and metallic purple on the nape of the neck. There is a bare patch of skin around the eye which is reddish in males but more yellow in females. The legs and base of the bill are also red, the rest of the bill being pale. Young birds are more ruddy than adults. The call is a repeated deep cooing, 'crooo, croo-

White-crowned Pigeon   **Red-necked Pigeon**

croo-croooo' with emphasis on the fourth syllable. It is slower and more emphatic than the previous species. There is also an alternative guttural rolled cooing note.

This species, though generally uncommon, is a widespread resident breeder in woodlands on the Virgin Islands and most of the Lesser Antilles (St Martin/Maarten, Saba, St Eustatius, Barbuda, Antigua, Montserrat, Guadeloupe, Dominica, Martinique, St Lucia, St Vincent, Barbados and Grenada). It is commonly hunted and in many regions has probably become rare for that reason. Although more common in rain forest, the species also occurs in drier lowland woodland. It nests mainly in trees, laying 1 – 2 white eggs between March and July. It feeds on the fruits and seeds of a wide variety of trees.

Zenaida Dove   *Zenaida aurita*
LENGTH: 28 – 30 cm (11 – 12 in)   LOCAL NAMES: Tourterelle, Wood
                                                Dove

This robust dove has reddish-brown upperparts with pink or cinnamon around the head, neck, and upper breast. The belly is pale grey-brown or white. There are two dark violet-blue streaks

Zenaida Dove   Common Ground-Dove

on the sides of the head and purple or violet on the sides of the
neck. The underparts can vary in hue from grey-brown or pink to
a deeper purple. The species may often be seen feeding in open areas
on the ground, and when flushed, its white-tipped outer tail feathers
are conspicuous. Otherwise, it frequently perches on trees or wires,
and its repetitive, gentle cooing 'coo-oo, coo, coo, coo' (the second
syllable rising sharply) is a familiar background sound in the dry
woodlands of the region.

The species occurs on most of the islands in the Eastern
Caribbean, though absent from St Vincent (except as a casual visitor
from the neighbouring Grenadines). It is found mainly in lowland
dry woodland and adjacent open country, although between March
and June some individuals move up into more mountainous
regions, and may enter rain forest. In Bridgetown, Barbados the
species even occurs along busy streets amongst buildings.

Breeding occurs mainly between February and August (though
it may occur at any time of year), with a clutch of two white eggs
laid in a flimsy nest of twigs built in a tree (for example logwood
Haematoxylum campechianum) or shrub, usually at a moderate

height but occasionally low down or even on the ground. Like other doves, it feeds mainly on seeds though it will also take fruits.

Eared or Violet-eared Dove   *Zenaida auriculata*
LENGTH: 22 – 25 cm (9 – 10 in)   LOCAL NAME: Tourterelle-Ortolan

The violet-eared dove is a terrestrial, stocky bird resembling the Zenaida dove but smaller with greyer upperparts, golden-bronze sides of the neck, and no white on the wings or tail. The male has a grey crown. Its call is a soft 'ooa-oo' or 'u-ooa-oo', similar to the Zenaida dove, although it does not make the more protracted cooing typical of that species and the **mourning dove** *Zenaida macroura* (a Greater Antillean species which occurs east to Culebra and Vieques).

It is a species of dry areas, occurring in open fields and scrub in the southern islands of the Eastern Caribbean. During this century it has spread north from continental South America, first being recorded in St Vincent in 1961 where it is still confined to the south-east of the island; and more recently, reaching the south end of St Lucia with casual records on Barbados and Martinique.

This species feeds mainly on seeds, and nests in trees or shrubs, laying two white eggs sometime between March and July.

Ground Dove, Common Ground-   *Columbina passerina*
Dove or Scaly-breasted Dove
LENGTH: 15 – 18 cm (6 – 7 in)   LOCAL NAME: Ortolan

This little ground-dove is common and widespread throughout the Eastern Caribbean. It is often to be seen on open ground, running along with head down picking up small seeds. The species is readily flushed, its bright rufous wing patches flashing as it makes short rapid flights. The rest of the body is greyish-brown with a short, rounded, dark brown tail. The breast may give a scaly appearance, caused by the dark centres of the feathers. The call is a long and monotonous series of low 'coo,coo,coo,coo', or a soft 'oo-ah', rising slightly at the end.

The species is found mainly in lowland open country and woodland. It usually nests on or close to the ground in a bush or tree, laying two white eggs in a nest of twigs and grasses mainly between March and July (though breeding may be extended from January to November).

71

Grenada Dove
LENGTH: 30 cm (12 in)

Leptotila wellsi

This species is confined to the island of Grenada with a total population of around 75 – 80 individuals (1989/90), concentrated mainly in dry scrub woodland in the south-west, between Lance aux Epines peninsula and Grande Anse village. It is a ground-dwelling dove, similar in size to the Zenaida dove but duller lacking any black or white markings on the wings, with no black spots on the sides of the head, and only a little white on the outer tail feathers. It has a white forehead and bare red skin around the eyes as in the red-necked pigeon. Its call is a plaintive, descending 'oooo', repeated at short intervals.

With such a perilously low population, the Grenada dove is clearly endangered, its main threat appearing to be nest predation from mongoose. Some authorities consider this a race of the South American grey-fronted dove *Leptotila rufaxilla*, but recent evidence has indicated that it is indeed a separate species.

Ruddy Quail-Dove
LENGTH: 25 – 30 cm (10 – 12 in)

Geotrygon montana

LOCAL NAMES: Perdrix, Partridge

A rather ugly looking dove, it is characterised by extensive bare red skin around the eyes, rufous (male) to olive-brown (female) upperparts, paler brown or buff underparts (washed with reddish-brown in the male). The bill and feet are reddish or orange. Its call

Ruddy Quail-Dove

is a prolonged booming sound like the distant blast of a foghorn but gradually fading away. It tends to live on the forest floor and is much more easily heard than seen.

The species occurs in the Greater Antilles east to Puerto Rico and Vieques Island (occurring only occasionally in the Virgin Islands, on St John although there has been a recent increase in sightings there). In the Lesser Antilles, it is found on Guadeloupe, Dominica, Martinique, St Lucia, St Vincent and Grenada. It is found mainly in rain forest at mid or high elevations although it will also occur in coastal dry scrub woodland and may undergo seasonal altitudinal movements. The loose nest of twigs and/or leaves is built low down in thick undergrowth, occasionally on the ground, and it is mainly on the ground or in the understorey that the species lives. Two pale buff eggs form the clutch, laid sometime between February and August.

Bridled Quail-Dove *Geotrygon mystacea*
LENGTH: 30 cm (12 in)   LOCAL NAMES: Perdrix Croissant, Partridge, Marmy Dove, Wood Dove, Wood Hen

The bridled quail-dove is similar to the previous species but most of the back is dark olive-brown with less distinct rufous areas on the wings and the outer tail feathers. The nape of the neck and mantle of the back are iridescent green and purple. There is a distinct whitish stripe below the eye and a pale throat, the rest of the underparts being buffish brown. The bill and legs are reddish or orange. The call is a mournful 'who-whooo' either on a single note or descending towards the end, with the middle of the second syllable being loudest before trailing off.

It occurs mainly in drier localities than the ruddy quail-dove, in lowland dry scrub woodland. It has a restricted distribution in the Eastern Caribbean, occurring on Vieques and possibly Culebra (east of Puerto Rico), the Virgin Islands (except Anegada and small cays), and the northern Lesser Antilles (Saba, St Eustatius, Antigua, Montserrat, Guadeloupe and Martinique; formerly Dominica, Barbuda), although rare or irregular in some of these. It is commonest on the larger Virgin Islands where numbers have increased since the early part of this century. However, elsewhere, the species appears to have declined and contracted its range and in the southern Antilles probably should now be considered under threat.

The nest, a flimsy platform of twigs/leaves, is built near the ground, with 1 – 2 pinkish buff eggs laid between March and August (but sometimes extending to December).

Imperial Parrot

PARROTS AND PARAKEETS *Psittacidae*

Imperial Parrot *Amazona imperialis*
LENGTH: 45 – 53 cm (18 – 20 in) LOCAL NAME: Sisserou

The largest of all *Amazona* parrots, this imposing bird has a dark green back and wings, a red speculum on each wing, and a bluish-purple head, neck, underparts and tail. There is also a thin red patch on the edge of the forewing. The eye is a conspicuous orange colour. Its call is a distinctive trumpeting, 'eeeee-er', usually with a falling inflection; also a wide variety of shrieks and whistles.

The imperial parrot is confined to the rain forest of northern Dominica, mainly on the slopes of Morne Diablotin above 500 m (1500 ft). It has seriously declined and contracted its range during this century. Initially probably affected by hunting, it suffered greatly from hurricanes David and Allen in 1979 and 1980, and from recent forest clearance in those areas bordering the protected northern forest reserve. There are presently only around 60 individuals remaining, although the species shows some signs of recovery. Nesting takes place high up in a cavity of a canopy tree, laying usually two white eggs between February and June. Like all the West Indian parrots, it feeds upon fruit, seeds and buds of a variety of forest trees (though taking more *Euterpe* palm fruits), and forages commonly in pairs which may aggregate to form small groups.

Red-necked Parrot *Amazona arausiaca*
LENGTH: 38 – 40 cm (15 – 16 in) LOCAL NAME: Jaco (Jacquot)

Another parrot species occurring in the mountains of northern Dominica, the red-necked parrot overlaps completely the range of the imperial, although it occurs also at lower altitudes down to 150 m (500 ft). It is also a rain forest species but less shy, tolerating human disturbance more readily. It has also declined in range and numbers during this century, for the same reasons as the previous species, and is rare in the southern half of the island. The present population numbers some 200 – 300 individuals, though it is fortunately showing signs of recovery and returning to areas it had vacated following the hurricanes.

The name of this species reflects a red patch it has on the under-surface of the neck although this may not always be distinct (see plate) and is not a good feature for separating it at a distance from the imperial parrot. Far more distinct is its much larger red

Red-necked Parrot

St Lucia Parrot

St Vincent Parrot

speculum on the wing, and greenish yellow tail. The head is also a violet blue, and the rest of the upperparts and the underparts are a brighter green. The call is a high-pitched harsh cry or squawk with little or no modulation.

Like its relative, the red-necked parrot nests high up in tree cavities of large forest trees, laying usually two white eggs between February and June. Its diet is also fruits, seeds and buds of a wide variety of trees.

St Lucia Parrot
LENGTH: 41 – 45 cm (16 – 18 in)

Amazona versicolor
LOCAL NAME: Jaco (Jacquot)

Like the red-necked parrot of Dominica, the St Lucia parrot is mainly green with a bluish head, red on the foreneck, a large red wing speculum and yellow tail. However, its underparts are more yellow-green, with patches of golden-brown or maroon over the breast. Its call is a harsh screech or shrill squawk.

The species is confined to the central mountain forests of St Lucia, within an area extending from Millet in the north, to Calfourc in the east, south to Piton Cochon, Piton St Esprit, Desrache and Grand Magazin. The population has previously suffered from hunting pressure, with habitat destruction by man and the recent hurricane Allen causing further declines. However, it appears to be recovering and presently numbers somewhere around 200 – 250 individuals, contained primarily within a forest reserve. Its nesting and feeding habits are similar to the previous two species.

St Vincent Parrot
LENGTH: 40 – 45 cm (16 – 18 cm)

Amazona guildingii
LOCAL NAME: Parrot

This is a very distinctive parrot, having a mainly white or yellow head with patches of violet on the sides and back of the head, wings of mainly golden brown but edged with green, a yellow speculum and purplish primaries. The back varies from golden-brown to green, the two extremes possibly representing separate morphs. The tail is green and violet-blue with a broad yellow band across the tip. Its calls are a range of loud squawks or creaking sounds.

The species is confined to the mountain forests of St Vincent, mainly in the Buccament, Cumberland and Wallilibou valleys. The present population numbers somewhere between 300 and 500 birds, and is threatened mainly from habitat loss and illegal capture of birds for the pet trade. Its nesting and feeding habits are similar to the other *Amazona* parrots described above.

Brown-throated or Caribbean Parakeet

Aratinga pertinax

LENGTH: 23 – 28 cm (9 – 11 in) LOCAL NAME: Parakeet

A small long-tailed member of the parrot family, the Caribbean parakeet was introduced to St Thomas (Virgin Islands) from Curaçao sometime in the last century, although it has expanded its range to Culebra (and Puerto Rico), and has been reported on Tortola and St John, whilst recently, individuals have also escaped from captivity in Dominica.

The species has a mainly green back and wings (with some blue on the edge of the primaries), and yellowish underparts. The forehead, sides of the head, throat and lower belly are orange-yellow. On take-off it commonly makes a shrill chattering call, typical of parakeets and may also utter a raucous squawk.

It occurs in dry scrub woodland and thicket, mainly on the eastern coastal slopes of St Thomas. It feeds on seeds and fruits of a variety of trees and shrubs, and nests in cavities of trees or active termite nests mainly between February and July (though possibly at any time of year). The normal clutch size is 4 – 7 chalky white eggs, and the species tends to nest colonially and move around in pairs or small flocks.

CUCKOOS AND ANIS

Cuculidae

Mangrove Cuckoo

Coccyzus minor

LENGTH: 28 – 30 cm (11 – 12 in) LOCAL NAMES: Coucou Manioc, Rain Bird, Cow Bird, Cat Bird, Dumb Bird, Coffin Bird

A large, relatively slender bird with a long tail, the mangrove cuckoo has grey-brown upperparts, and a white throat becoming buffish on the breast and particularly the belly. A black stripe goes through the eye to the ear coverts. The bill is curved, with a dark upper mandible and yellow or orange lower mandible, tipped with black. The tail broadens towards the end before tapering at the tip. The outer tail feathers are black with contrasting white spots at the tips, giving a banded appearance to the undersurface of the tail. The buff feathers on the underparts extend onto the upper legs.

This species is widely distributed at low densities in the Eastern Caribbean, occurring as a breeding resident in the Virgin Islands and the Lesser Antilles from Barbuda, Antigua and Montserrat south (except Barbados). Although a bird mainly of mangrove and

Mangrove Cuckoo   **Yellow-billed Cuckoo**

dry scrub woodland, the species is also found on the edge of rain forest, in secondary and riverine vegetation, and even alongside cultivation. Although not a shy species, it is relatively inconspicuous, occurring usually in thick vegetation and making only short flights. Its presence is usually revealed by its guttural call, 'ka-ka-ka-ka-ka-kow-kow-kow' repeated intermittently.

Unlike Old World cuckoos, the mangrove cuckoo lays 2 – 3 bluish-green eggs in its own nest, built of twigs in thick vegetation. The breeding season appears to be mainly March to August. Its diet is mainly lizards, insects and spiders.

Yellow-billed Cuckoo   *Coccyzus americanus*
LENGTH: 28 – 30 cm (11 – 12 in)   LOCAL NAMES: Rain Bird, Rain Crow

Resembling the mangrove cuckoo, this species is best distinguished by its white underparts lacking any buff, its lack of black on the side of the face, and more obvious yellow lower mandible. In flight, the rufous patches on the outer edges of the upperwing may be observed. Its call is higher-pitched and less guttural than the

79

mangrove cuckoo, ending in a more deliberate 'kow-kow-kow' or 'kowp-kowp-kowp'.

The yellow-billed cuckoo is a rare breeder in the Greater Antilles (Puerto Rico and St Croix) and on St Kitts, but elsewhere in the Virgin Islands and the Lesser Antilles it generally occurs as a relatively uncommon passage migrant or winter visitor (most common in October – November). It occupies similar habitat to the previous species, occurring primarily in lowland dry scrub woodland. A flimsy nest of sticks is made in which 2 – 5 blue eggs are laid mainly between May and July. Like the previous species, it feeds primarily upon lizards, insects and spiders.

Smooth-billed Ani

LENGTH: 30 – 35 cm (12 – 14 in)

Crotophaga ani

LOCAL NAMES: Merle Corbeau, Blackbird, Black Witch, Black Parrot, Black Daw, Tick Bird

This very distinctive all-black cuckoo has a very large deep, curved bill, short rounded wings and a long tail, which, like other cuckoos, broadens towards the end before tapering at the tip. Its call is a

Smooth-billed Ani

shrill 'wer-ik, wer-ik', often uttered by members of the group as they fly with alternate glides across open country.

The species is widespread in South America and the Caribbean, and in the region under consideration, breeds in the Virgin Islands and Lesser Antilles from St Eustatius and Montserrat southward (except Martinique and Barbados). It is a bird of open country, following the spread of plantations up into mountainous rain forest areas. A large bulky nest of sticks is made collectively, in the centre of a bush or tree, and into this several families lay their eggs. Clutch sizes can sometimes number 20 or more, laid in layers of 4 – 5 eggs separated by leaves. Only the upper eggs hatch and members of the group then cooperate in rearing the young. Breeding occurs mainly between March and July although it can take place at any time of year. The diet includes fruit and lizards but mainly comprises insects such as grasshoppers, beetles, dragonflies and butterflies. These are taken from the ground or low vegetation, and the species often feeds on insects disturbed by grazing cattle.

BARN OWLS *Tytonidae*

Barn Owl *Tyto alba*
LENGTH: 30 – 38 cm (12 – 15 in)   LOCAL NAMES: Chat-huant, Jumbie Bird, Screech Owl

The barn owl is one of the few nocturnal birds to occur in the Eastern Caribbean, where it is found only on the Lesser Antillean islands of Dominica, St Vincent, the Grenadines and Grenada. It has a heart-shaped pale face with short curved beak, light brown head, but dark grey or brown back and wings. The breast and belly are also quite dark in these populations, ranging from fawn to buffish. Its cry is a piercing scream, although a loud clicking sound may also be made.

The species nests in caves, tree cavities and in old buildings, laying up to eight white eggs anytime between February and September. It feeds on bats and small rodents, hunting over open ground in almost any habitat.

Barn Owl

TYPICAL OWLS

Strigidae

Puerto Rican Screech Owl
LENGTH: 23 – 25 cm (9 – 10 in)

Otus nudipes
LOCAL NAME: Cuckoo Bird

The only small owl occurring in the Eastern Caribbean, this species is now extremely rare (possibly extirpated) in the Virgin Islands where in the past it has been recorded on St Thomas, St John, St Croix, Virgin Gorda and Tortola. Elsewhere it is only found in Puerto Rico where it is a common resident. On that island, it occurs in a variety of wooded areas from dense forests and coffee plantations in the mountains to isolated thickets on the coast. Being entirely nocturnal, it is rarely seen, although it can be attracted by imitating the squeaking of a mouse.

The species is greyish-brown above and white below but with heavy brown or black streaks. Some birds may be distinctly rufous. Unlike some other screech owls, the species lacks ear-tufts. It utters a number of sounds mainly in the evening or early morning. These range from a loud tremulous trill, various chattering or whoops, a loud 'coo-coo', or occasionally a hoarse croaking or laugh.

Nesting occurs between April and June when two white eggs are laid in a tree cavity. Its diet is exclusively animals, including various insects.

NIGHTJARS

Caprimulgidae

St Lucia Nightjar
LENGTH: 28 cm (11 in)

Caprimulgus otiosus
LOCAL NAME: Jacques-papa-pau

This Venezuelan nightjar, considered by some authorities to be conspecific with the rufous nightjar *Caprimulgus rufus* occurs in the Eastern Caribbean only on St Lucia, where it may be found in dry scrub woodland at Grande Anse, Caille Des, Louvet, Mal y bon and near Petite Anse river (and possibly elsewhere). It is a reddish-brown bird, barred, streaked and spotted with black. Like other nightjars it has a large flat head, small bill, long rounded tail and broad wings. Its repeated nocturnal call gives rise to the local name 'Jacques-papa-pau', the accent being on the fourth syllable. This distinctive call is the basis for considering it a separate species. It nests on the ground, laying 2 indistinctly spotted eggs probably mainly between April and July. Feeding on insects occurs particularly at dusk, and like other nightjars it is inactive during the day.

Another South American species, the **white-tailed nightjar** *Caprimulgus cayennensis*, occurs on the lowland grassy slopes and

St Lucia Nightjar   **Lesser Antillean Swift**

scrub of southern Martinique and in Barbados. It is 5 cm (2 in)
smaller than the St Lucia nightjar, and the male is strikingly
marked with a white band across the wings and mostly white outer
tail feathers. Females are browner with no white on the wings or
tail, but with brownish-yellow spots on the primaries. Its call is
a plaintive, high-pitched whistle. Nesting and feeding habits are
similar to the previous species.

Common Nighthawk   *Chordeiles minor*
LENGTH: 20 – 25 cm (8 – 10 in)   LOCAL NAMES: Mosquito Hawk,
Piramidig

The most characteristic feature of this species is the long white-
banded wings. In the male the slightly forked tail has a white band.
The nighthawk is most commonly seen at or just before dusk,
hunting fairly high in the air for insects. Its call is also distinctive,
a nasal 'peent'. The species occurs regularly in spring or autumn
in the Virgin Islands (St Croix and St John; occasionally elsewhere)
but is only a casual migrant to the Lesser Antilles.

84

Antillean or West Indian Nighthawk   *Chordeiles gundlachii*
LENGTH: 20 – 25 cm (8 – 10 in)   LOCAL NAMES: Mosquito Hawk, Piramidig

This species was previously considered a race of the common nighthawk. It is almost indistinguishable from it, and has the distinctive long, pointed wings with bold white bar, erratic flight and slightly forked tail (banded in the male). Its call is a loud, rasping 'que-re-que-que' or 'pity-pit-pit' and this is the best way to distinguish it from the previous species.

The Antillean nighthawk is an uncommon summer resident (mainly May – September) breeding in the Virgin Islands (and Puerto Rico). Eastward migration may take place between August and early September, and it is possible that nighthawks seen at this time, previously identified as common nighthawk, may be of this species. Specific field identification can only really be made on the basis of call. One, occasionally two, bluish eggs (heavily splotched with brown markings) are laid directly on the open ground in an open area in May or June. The species is most often seen at or just before dusk when it feeds upon flying insects high above fields and pastures.

SWIFTS   *Apodidae*

Lesser Antillean Swift   *Chaetura martinica*
LENGTH: 10 – 13 cm (4 – 5 in)   LOCAL NAMES: Hirondelle, Rain Bird

A small ashy grey swift, this species is confined to the Lesser Antilles, breeding on Guadeloupe, Dominica, Martinique, St Lucia and St Vincent. It has a fluttering flight and may usually be seen in large groups above ravines and open ground mainly in forested mountain regions. The species has a chittering call. It probably nests mainly in hollow trees, and perhaps also caves, with breeding thought to take place mainly between March and July.

A close relative, the **gray-rumped swift** *Chaetura cinereiventris* replaces this species in the forested hills of Grenada. It is very similar in appearance but has more glossy black upperparts giving greater contrast with the ashy grey rump and underparts.
Finally, another similar small black swift, the **short-tailed swift** *Chaetura brachyura*, occurs in St Vincent. Although most common in lowland areas, it is also found in mountain valleys. This species has longer wings than the Lesser Antillean swift, emphasised further by its shorter tail. Otherwise, it has a pale grey rump, tail

and undertail coverts, contrasting with the rest of the plumage which is blackish. The species has been noted nesting in abandoned chimneys of sugar cane factories. It may be a partial migrant, being virtually absent between October and February.

Black Swift
LENGTH: 15 – 18 cm (6 – 7 in)

Cypseloides niger
LOCAL NAMES: Swallow, Oiseau de la Pluie

The black swift has sooty black upperparts, slightly paler underparts, a shallow forked tail, and long rounded wings reminiscent of the European swift. It occurs as a summer resident (between March and November) in St Kitts, nesting in various Lesser Antillean islands from Guadeloupe to St Vincent (excepting Barbados), but is accidental in the Virgin Islands. The species occurs mainly over forests or adjacent open areas in more mountainous regions where it can be seen dashing across the sky after insects, uttering soft 'tchip, tchip' calls. During rainy weather, it will move into lowland areas to feed. It nests colonially on ledges and in holes of cliffs, mainly between April and August. The nest is a shallow cup of moss into which a single large white egg is laid.

HUMMINGBIRDS

Trochilidae

Purple-throated Carib
LENGTH: 12 cm (5 in)

Eulampis jugularis
LOCAL NAMES: Colibri, Colibri Madère, Doctor Bird

A relatively large, dark hummingbird, this species has an iridescent purple throat although this shows up only with direct sunlight, otherwise appearing black. The wings are metallic green sometimes with a blue iridescent patch on the coverts. The rest of the body and tail are dark except for the rump and undertail coverts which are bluish green. The curved dark bill is longer in the female, which is also smaller in size, shorter winged and with a usually duller purple throat, though otherwise similar to the male. Its call is a sharp 'chewp' note, sometimes repeated rapidly one or two times.

The purple-throated carib is widespread in the Lesser Antilles from Saba to St Vincent (except Barbuda, Désirade, Iles des Saintes, Bequia and Barbados where it is only a casual visitor). Recently, there has also been a record from St John (Virgin Islands). Although more common in humid forest and adjacent plantations, the species

Purple-throated Carib

Green-throated Carib

Antillean Crested Hummingbird

will also occur in small numbers in lowland dry forest. It feeds both in the canopy and understorey and may often be seen dashing past like a torpedo on wings, uttering ticking alarm notes. Its diet includes a lot of insects as well as nectar from a variety of flowering plants. Breeding takes place mainly between March and July and the cup-shaped nest is often hung from small branches high above the ground, the usual clutch being of two white eggs.

Green-throated Carib — *Sericotes holosericeus*
LENGTH: 11 – 12 cm (4½ – 5 in)   LOCAL NAMES: Colibri Vert, Green Doctor Bird

Slightly smaller than the preceding species, the green-throated carib is green all over except for a patch of violet-blue on the breast and a violet-black tail. The green underparts darken towards the tail. The female is smaller and shorter winged than the male but has a longer, more curved bill. The call is a sharp 'chewp', and there is also a loud wing rattle.

This species is common in the Virgin Islands and throughout the Lesser Antilles (except for the southernmost Grenadines). It is a bird primarily of lowland dry woodland, garden, and cultivation but will also occur uncommonly in mountain regions where open areas such as citrus plantations exist. Its feeding habits are broadly similar to the purple-throated carib, and it may be seen alongside that species. Breeding takes place mainly between March and June when two white eggs are laid in a downy nest lined with grasses and lichens.

Antillean Crested Hummingbird — *Orthorhyncus cristatus*
LENGTH: 8 – 9 cm (3½ in)   LOCAL NAMES: Frou-frou, Little Doctor Bird

A tiny hummingbird weighing little more than two grams, this species is mainly green above and grey below with a short straight bill and a green and blue iridescent crest (most pronounced in the male). The sexes are broadly similar although the male has darker underparts with some green. Its call is an emphatic 'pit-chew'.

The Antillean crested hummingbird is one of the commonest of Eastern Caribbean birds, occurring in the Virgin Islands and throughout the Lesser Antilles. It may be found in all habitats and from sea level to the tops of the highest mountains. Breeding takes place between February and July when two white eggs are laid in

Male Blue-headed Hummingbird

Female Blue-headed Hummingbird

a tiny cup-shaped nest of grass fibres and lichens, which is generally placed in shrubs or herbaceous vegetation near the ground. It feeds primarily on nectar from a wide variety of flowering plants (from herbs to tall trees).

Blue-headed Hummingbird *Cyanophaia bicolor*
LENGTH: 11 cm (4½ in)   LOCAL NAMES: Frou-frou bleu, Colibri Tête-bleu

The male of this beautiful little hummingbird has a blue head, back and wings, with blue extending onto the throat and breast. The rest of the underparts are green, tinged in areas with blue, and the flanks are often green towards the nape of the neck. The lower mandible of its straight bill is pink with a black tip. The female is strikingly different, having mainly green upperparts tinged in patches with blue. The outer tail feathers are also mainly blue but are tipped with white. The central tail feathers are tipped with dark blue. The throat, breast and belly are all white contrasting strongly with the green back.

The blue-headed hummingbird is found in rain forest and elfin woodland in the mountains of Dominica and Martinique. Although usually found above 600 m (1800 ft), where suitable habitat exists the species can also be seen in lowland areas. It feeds on nectar (and small insects) from the flowers of understorey shrubs and herbs near ground level. It builds a tiny cup-shaped nest of herbs, mosses and lichens, usually low down on a fern or hanging from the fronds of a palm. Two tiny white eggs are laid mainly between February and May.

Rufous-breasted Hermit *Glaucis hirsuta*
LENGTH: 12 cm (5 in)   LOCAL NAME: Brown Doctor Bird

A large hummingbird, the rufous-throated hermit has a rather long curved bill with a yellow lower mandible. It is mainly green above and brown below, although more rufous in the female. Most of the tail is chestnut brown with a band of black just behind conspicuous white tips. This South American species occurs in the Lesser Antilles only on Grenada where it is found particularly in rain forest above about 450 m (1500 ft). It normally feeds well below the canopy, and on this island seems to take the place of the purple-throated carib.

It feeds mainly on nectar but will also take small insects and spiders. Its flimsy nest is often attached to the underside of a fern, herb or low shrub, often above a bank or stream edge.

Antillean Mango
LENGTH: 11 – 12 cm (4½ – 5 in)

Anthracothorax dominicus
LOCAL NAME: Doctor Bird

This relatively large hummingbird has light yellowish-green upper-parts and mainly blackish (male) or greyish-white (female) under-parts. The outer tail feathers of the female are brownish-grey tipped with white. The bill is curved. Young males resemble females but quickly show traces of black on the underparts. Its call is an unmusical, thin but loud, trill and it will also make a series of sharp chipping notes.

Although the Antillean mango is the commonest large humming-bird in the lowlands of Puerto Rico, it has become extremely rare in the Virgin Islands, no longer occurring on most (for example St John) and possibly remaining only in small numbers on Anegada and St Thomas. The cause of the decline is thought to be competition with the green-throated carib which has been expanding its range west in the Greater Antilles. Its diet includes nectar from a variety of flowering plants. A deep downy cup-shaped nest is built into which two white eggs are laid mainly between March and August.

KINGFISHERS
Alcedinidae

Ringed Kingfisher
LENGTH: 38 – 40 cm (15 – 16 in)

Ceryle torquata
LOCAL NAMES: Kingfisher, Cra-cra

This large, strikingly coloured crested kingfisher has a heavy bill with chestnut (male) or blue-grey spotted with white (female) upper breast, a chestnut belly and undertail coverts. The head, back and wings are blue with a broad white band around the neck and often a white spot near the eye. The tail is banded black and white. The call is a loud, harsh rattle, reminiscent of a maniacal laugh.

The ringed kingfisher is widespread in Central and South America, but in the Eastern Caribbean it occurs only on the Lesser Antillean islands of Guadeloupe and Dominica (and Trinidad). It is uncommon, mainly near freshwater streams, lakes and montane swamps although it may also be found on the coast where streams/rivers enter the sea. Like most kingfishers, it feeds upon

Ringed Kingfisher

Belted Kingfisher

fish captured by plunge diving, and nests in a burrow usually excavated in a bank, laying three white eggs. The breeding season is mainly between March and July.

Belted Kingfisher
LENGTH: 30 – 33 cm (12 – 13 in)

Ceryle alcyon
LOCAL NAMES: Kingfisher, Martin-pêcheur

Another crested kingfisher, this species is smaller than the previous one and lacks any chestnut on the belly or undertail coverts. Both sexes have a blue head, back and wings and a blue band across the upper breast. The rest of the underparts are white and, like the ringed kingfisher, there is a white band around the neck. The female differs from the male in having a narrow band of chestnut across the lower breast. The blue wings are spotted with white and the tail banded black and white.

Kingfishers are easily recognised in flight by their relatively large head, and deep, irregular wingbeats. The call is a harsh rattle, less modulated in the belted than the ringed kingfisher.

The belted kingfisher breeds in North America and winters in Central America and northern South America. It occurs throughout the Eastern Caribbean mainly between October and April although individuals may be seen in all months of the year. It favours coastal areas, lowland rivers, lakes and lagoons, where it may be seen on a conspicuous perch before calling and flying out over water in search of food. It frequently hovers stationary in mid-air before plunge-diving into the water after a fish.

WOODPECKERS   *Picidae*

Guadeloupe Woodpecker   *Melanerpes herminieri*
LENGTH: 25 – 29 cm (10 – 11½ in)   LOCAL NAME: Tapeur

The only woodpecker breeding in the Lesser Antilles, this species is confined to the island of Guadeloupe where it occurs mainly in humid forest of eastern Basse Terre, between 100 and 700 m. It is rare in drier areas of its western slopes and found in only a few wooded areas on Grande Terre. It has an all-black appearance although close-up the underparts have a reddish hue.

Like all woodpeckers,the species may be seen typically climbing up the trunks of trees using its stiff pointed tail for support. It feeds on insects obtained from the bark, flying off with characteristic undulating flight. It nests in a hole excavated in a tree.

Yellow-bellied Sapsucker   *Sphyrapicus varius*
LENGTH: 20 – 22 cm (8 – 8½ in)

This small woodpecker has black upperparts mottled with white on the back and wings,and has a conspicuous white wing patch. The male has a red chin and throat, which are white in the female. Both sexes have a red forehead. Immatures are dull brown but share the white wing patch of adults. It is usually silent during winter but otherwise may utter a querulous 'mew'.

It is a rare winter visitor to the Virgin Islands between October and April, occurring mainly in sparsely wooded areas. Otherwise it has been recorded in the Lesser Antilles only as an accidental visitor.

TYRANT FLYCATCHERS — *Tyrannidae*

Gray Kingbird — *Tyrannus dominicensis*

LENGTH: 23 – 24 cm (9 – 9½ in)   LOCAL NAMES: Pipiri, Pitiwick, Chichery, Chinchery, Rain Bird

This is the largest of the tyrant flycatchers in the Eastern Caribbean. It is grey above and white below with a black stripe on the side of the head from the base of the bill to the ear coverts. The black bill is large, and like other tyrant flycatchers, it is flattened with a wide base and hooked tip. Some of the feathers in the crown are orange although this is usually only visible when the bird is in the hand.

The gray kingbird occurs throughout the Eastern Caribbean where it is a conspicuous bird of open country, perching on exposed branches or wires from which it makes frequent sallies into the air to catch large flying insects. Sometimes it will also take insects from ground vegetation. Its call is a high-pitched, rather harsh 'pecherie' or 'pitirre'.

The species builds an open nest loosely constructed of twigs high up in a tree, laying 2 – 4 reddish eggs (heavily splotched at one end) usually between March and July. After the nesting season, numbers

Gray Kingbird

may be seen congregating on wires in lowland areas, dispersing or partially migrating off the island.

Tropical Kingbird
Tyrannus melancholicus

LENGTH: 22 cm (9 in)   LOCAL NAMES: Yellow Pipiri, Pipiri Jaune

Similar to the previous species, the tropical kingbird is distinguished by having an olive-green back and grey or greenish-yellow breast becoming bright yellow on the belly. Although occurring from the southern United States to South America, this open country species breeds in the Eastern Caribbean region only on Grenada (also Trinidad & Tobago) where it was very rare and may have ceased to breed. Its call is a similar, though softer, high-pitched twittering. Feeding and nesting habits are similar to the gray kingbird.

Fork-tailed Flycatcher
Tyrannus savana

LENGTH: 25 – 40 cm (10 – 16 in)   LOCAL NAME: Scissors-tail

This South American species has a black head, grey back and wings, white underparts and an extremely long forked black tail. The outer tail feathers are longer in the male (28 cm, 11 in) than in females and immatures (18 cm, 7 in). The fork-tailed flycatcher occurs in the Eastern Caribbean only on Grenada and Barbados where it is a winter visitor of open country. It is a gregarious species, gathering in large groups to roost often in mangroves. It feeds on insects and fruits such as those of the Royal Palm.

Lesser Antillean or Ober's Flycatcher
Myiarchus oberi

LENGTH: 18 – 19 cm (7½ – 8 in)   LOCAL NAMES: Gobe-mouches Huppé, Janeau, Pipiri Gros-tête

A rather attractive flycatcher, this species has brown upperparts, a pale grey throat and upper breast, becoming lemon yellow on the belly. In several island forms, the wings and tail are edged with rufous whilst the amount of yellow on the underparts may also vary. The commonest call is a prolonged rather pure plaintive whistle, although other calls often made at dawn may be a series of short modulated whistles, 'oo-ee', 'ee-oo' or 'e-oo-ee'.

It is a Lesser Antillean species of woodland edge or adjacent tree plantations, mainly in more humid areas, occurring on St Kitts,

Lesser Antillean Flycatcher

Nevis, Barbuda, Montserrat, Guadeloupe, Dominica, Martinique and St Lucia. Feeding generally takes place near or at ground level, with insects snatched from the air or from low vegetation. The species has a varied diet which includes not only flying beetles and crickets, but also small frogs and berries. Breeding occurs between March and July with 2 – 4 spotted eggs laid in a twig nest often in the hole of a tree.

Grenada Flycatcher
LENGTH: 20 cm (8 in)

Myiarchus nugator

LOCAL NAMES: Loggerhead, Sunset Bird

Very similar to the Lesser Antillean flycatcher, this species replaces the previous one on Grenada, St Vincent and the Grenadines. It was previously considered a subspecies of the rusty-tailed flycatcher *Myiarchus tyrannulus* of the southern United States and South America. It has a much harsher call, 'queuk, queuk' and a loud 'quip'. It is distinguished from *M. oberi* by having secondaries fringed with grey or cream rather than rufous, and from both species by the inside of its mouth being bright orange rather than pale yellow. The species is fairly common in lightly wooded country and along the forest edge, mainly in lowland areas. It feeds on insects and fruits, and breeds between March and July in tree cavities, building a nest mainly of sticks and leaves.

Puerto Rican Flycatcher
LENGTH: 18 – 20 cm (7 – 8 in)

Myiarchus antillarum

LOCAL NAME: Jüi

Another species similar and closely related to the Lesser Antillean flycatcher, it is distinguished by its white abdomen and lack of cinnamon in the tail. It has a fairly prolonged, plaintive, whistle, characterised as 'jui' or 'whee', and often dropping in frequency. Other calls include a two-syllabled 'wick-up', a series of emphatic 'huit, huit' notes, a rolling 'pee-r-r-r', and a rasping note. There is also a dawn song 'whee-a-wit-whee'.

This species occurs in wooded areas of St Thomas and St John, Virgin Gorda and Tortola (Virgin Islands) as well as Puerto Rico and the islands of Vieques and Culebra east of there. Habitat destruction by man and hurricanes reduced the species to near extinction in the 1930s and now it is rare everywhere except Puerto Rico. Its feeding and nesting habits are similar to the Lesser Antillean flycatcher. Three to four spotted, yellowish-white eggs are laid in a tree hole nest between late April and July.

Lesser Antillean Pewee

Lesser Antillean Pewee *Contopus latirostris*
LENGTH: 15 cm (6 in)   LOCAL NAMES: Gobe-mouches, Jüi Pequeño, Bobito

A small flycatcher with grey-brown upperparts, greyish-white throat and breast merging into a light buff belly (more rufous in birds from St Lucia). It has a small, broad flat bill, with a tuft of bristles at the base. The lower mandible is mainly yellow, the upper mandible black. Its call is distinctive, either a loud trill 'preee-e-e' or a high-pitched 'peet-peet-peet-peet'.

This pewee is confined to the Lesser Antillean islands of Guadeloupe, Dominica, Martinique and St Lucia (also western Puerto Rico), occurring at low densities mainly in rain forest clearings and adjacent citrus or coffee plantations. It is a confiding species of the understorey, possibly making use of humans to flycatch small insects disturbed by them. It makes a small cup-shaped nest often in the fork of a tree, laying two or three spotted, cream-coloured eggs between March and June.

Caribbean Elaenia

Caribbean Elaenia
LENGTH: 16 – 18 cm (6 – 7 in)

Elaenia martinica
LOCAL NAMES: Siffleur, Jüi Blanco, Pee-whistler

This is by far the commonest of flycatchers in the region, occurring throughout the Eastern Caribbean (except some of the Grenadines). It is found in virtually all habitats except in dense rain forest.

It is a rather plain grey bird with two greyish-white wing-bars, and an often inconspicuous patch of white on the crown. The underparts are paler grey, in some populations the belly washed with yellow. The bill is small, black and narrower than other flycatchers described above. Its call is a harsh, repetitive 'che-up', often followed by 'wi-wi-yup'.

The species feeds on insects and small berries, both usually taken from around or just below the canopy. It builds a rough cup-shaped nest in a tree or shrub, laying 2 – 3 spotted eggs (pinkish with lilac and brown markings), mainly between March and July.

Yellow-bellied Elaenia

LENGTH: 16 cm (6 in)

Elaenia flavogaster

LOCAL NAME: Topknot Pipiri

Although closely resembling the Caribbean elaenia, this species has a distinctly lemon yellow belly and usually a prominent crest. Its call is also distinctive: a harsh 'creup-wi-creup' or a simple drawn-out 'creup'. It is widespread in Central and South America. In the Eastern Caribbean it occurs amongst open country in the lowlands of St Vincent, the Grenadines and Grenada. Like the previous species with which it overlaps on St Vincent, it feeds on insects and small berries. The more substantial nest is lined with feathers and 2 – 3 heavily spotted eggs are laid between March and July.

SWALLOWS

Hirundinidae

Caribbean Martin

LENGTH: 18 – 20 cm (7 – 8 in)

Progne dominicensis

LOCAL NAMES: Swallow, Hirondelle, Gale Bird

This large swallow has glossy very dark blue upperparts, often with white on the nape or sides of the head, and pale underparts. Females and immatures are duller brown, with greyish brown throat, breast and flanks and a white belly. The species has broader wings and more soaring flight than other swallows. The song is a low-pitched liquid, rolling twitter, and calls include a short 'chu' or 'chu-chu'. The taxonomic status of this newly recognised species and the North American **purple martin** *Progne subis* is still unclear and may in fact represent different morphs. The latter is separated on the basis of an all dark belly (glossy purple in the male; brown in females and immatures). The Caribbean martin is a locally common summer resident throughout the Eastern Caribbean, leaving in October or November to spend the winter in South America before returning again the following February or March. Some individuals may remain through the year. It occurs mainly in towns, open country, and along sea-cliffs, nesting in colonies under the eaves of a building, inside caves or in cliff crevices. 3 – 6 white eggs are laid sometime between March and July.

Caribbean Martin   Barn Swallow

Barn Swallow   *Hirundo rustica*
LENGTH: 15 – 19 cm (6 – 7½ in)

Adult barn swallows are glossy blue with a chestnut forehead and rusty underparts, a white rump and a deeply forked tail (except in moult). Immatures also do not have a deeply forked tail and the underparts are bicoloured, with a blackish breast and white belly, and white spots on the tail. This species is a common passage migrant (mainly August – October) and winter visitor throughout the Eastern Caribbean, most individuals being immature. They are most often seen over lowland open country, on wires along roadsides or above coastal swamp or lakes.

Another regular though uncommon passage migrant and winter visitor is the **bank swallow** or **sand martin** *Riparia riparia*. It is a small grey-brown swallow with a shallow forked tail and a blackish breast band across its white underparts.

Cliff Swallow   *Hirundo (= Petrochelidon) pyrrhonota*
LENGTH: 13 – 15 cm (5 – 6 in)   LOCAL NAME: Hirondelle

This species is a rare migrant and winter visitor to the Eastern Caribbean. It has a much squarer tail than the barn swallow, with a whitish forehead, dark chestnut sides of the head and throat, and black patch on the foreneck. The broad martin-like wings are brown and the rump is orange. It occurs over open country, around towns and along the coast.

WRENS   *Troglodytidae*

House Wren   *Troglodytes aedon*
LENGTH: 12 – 13 cm (4½ – 5 in)   LOCAL NAMES: Rossignol, Oiseau Bon Dieu, Rock Bird, Wall Bird

This small brown bird has black bars on its wings and tail, an indistinct pale stripe above the eye, and a relatively long tail which it sometimes cocks upwards in the manner typical of wrens. Populations from St Lucia and St Vincent have whiter underparts than elsewhere. Like other wrens, the species has a rich, loud bubbling song which can be very variable.

    Although widespread in continental America, in the Caribbean it is confined to the islands of Guadeloupe, Dominica, St Lucia, St Vincent and Grenada. It is common and widespread only on Dominica and Grenada. This fragmented distribution may be the result of nest predation by the introduced mongoose. It is a species of undergrowth particularly in or adjacent to rain forest although on St Lucia it is apparently confined to dry woodland in the lowlands of the north-east (particularly Petite Anse Valley). It feeds mainly on insects but will also take small lizards. Breeding occurs between March and August. Usually 3 – 5 speckled eggs are laid in a hole or domed nest commonly built in a bank or tree stump, sometimes in a crevice of a wall or building.

House Wren

SOLITAIRES, THRUSHES AND ALLIES *Turdinae*

Rufous-throated Solitaire *Myadestes genibarbis*
LENGTH: 19 – 20 cm (7½ – 8 in)   LOCAL NAMES: Siffleur Montagne,
Mountain Whistler, Soufrière Bird

A very attractive small thrush, the rufous-throated solitaire has a slate-grey head and back, dark grey wings and tail with white outer tail feathers. The underparts are mainly pale grey but with rufous-orange on the throat, lower belly and undertail coverts. The bill is small and black, and the legs are yellow-orange. Birds in St Vincent are black above with a greyish-olive rump.

Many island legends speak of the mountain whistler, a spirit that no one ever sees but only hears calling across mountain valleys. This is the solitaire whose song is so much more frequently heard than its owner is seen. The song, likened to a creaking gate, is a prolonged plaintive whistle. It is sometimes uttered on a single note or, particularly during the breeding season, as a double whistle, the second note either higher or lower than the first.

Rufous-throated Solitaire

The species occurs in Dominica, Martinique, St Lucia and St Vincent (also Jamaica and Hispaniola). It is found mainly in mountain rain forest and feeds on small berries and also insects. It breeds between March and July, building a cup-shaped nest in a variety of sites – steep banks above streams, in the heart of a bromeliad or tree fern, among vines or in a tree. Two bluish-white spotted eggs are laid.

Bare-eyed Thrush　　　　　　　　　　*Turdus nudigenis*
LENGTH: 23 – 24 cm (9 – 9½ in)　LOCAL NAMES: Yellow-eyed Grive,
　　　　　　　　　　　　　　　　Grive à Paupières Jaunes

The bare-eyed thrush is a South American species which occurs in the Eastern Caribbean only in the southern Lesser Antilles (Martinique to Grenada except Barbados) and Trinidad and Tobago. It is thought to be a recent colonist to islands north of St Vincent. It is fairly common in lowlands around settlements and cultivation, in woodland and gardens.

The species is uniformly dark greyish-olive above and brownish-grey below but with a darker, streaked throat. Its name derives from a very distinctive bare yellow patch around the eye. The song is a clear monotonously repeated 'ture-too-too', similar to an American robin. It also makes a cat-like 'keer-lee' mewing sound in alarm. It feeds on fruit and insects mainly taken from the ground, and builds a substantial cup-shaped nest at a moderate height in the fork of a tree, laying 2 – 3 blue spotted eggs. Breeding occurs between March and July.

Cocoa Thrush *Turdus fumigatus*
LENGTH: 23 – 24 cm (9 – 9½ in)   LOCAL NAMES: Mountain Grive, Black-eyed Grive

Similar to the bare-eyed thrush, this South American species, however, has much darker reddish-brown underparts and no yellow around the eye. Its song is plaintive and it has a loud nasal 'wheeo-wheeo-wheeo' call. It is found in mountain forest and adjacent clearings or plantations on St Vincent and Grenada, otherwise occurring in the Caribbean only in the lowlands of Trinidad. It feeds on insects and fruit, and builds a mossy nest in a tree, laying 2 – 3 greenish-blue spotted eggs around March to July.

Red-legged Thrush *Turdus (= Mimocichla) plumbeus*
LENGTH: 25 – 28 cm (10 – 11 in)   LOCAL NAMES: Zorzal Azul, Ouète-ouète, Pierrot Vantard

Although this species occurs on a number of islands in the Greater Antilles including Puerto Rico (but not the Virgin Islands), it is found in the Lesser Antilles only on Dominica. It is a striking bird with a slate-grey back, black tail with white tips to the outer tail feathers, and an orange-red bill and legs. The chin and throat are white with vertical black stripes, the rest of the underparts being greyish or white. There is also a narrow orange band of bare skin around the eye. Immatures have browner upperparts. The call is a loud 'wet-wet' and the song a prolonged series of rather thin notes made up of phrases of 1 – 3 syllables.

The species occurs mainly in lowland dry woodland although it will also visit wooded plantations and, outside the breeding season, may move up into rain forest edge. In the Greater Antilles it may also be found in gardens. It feeds on insects taken near or at ground level, as well as a variety of small fruits. Breeding occurs

Red-legged Thrush

Forest Thrush

Tropical Mockingbird

mainly between April and July with a bulky cup-shaped nest built in a bush or tree, into which 2 – 4 pale green or whitish spotted eggs are laid.

Forest Thrush
LENGTH: 25 – 28 cm (10 – 11 in)

Cichlherminia lherminieri
LOCAL NAME: Grive à Pieds Jaunes

The forest thrush is a large, stocky bird with a dark brown back, black and chestnut-brown spots over the breast, and white belly and undertail coverts. The bill and legs are yellow, and there is a conspicuous bare yellow patch around the eye. There is just a small amount of white in the wing along the leading edge, and only a little white in the tail. The species is very secretive, dashing through the understorey at high speed. The song is a very pure cadence of notes, relatively loud and far-carrying. The call is a very loud, abrupt 'chuck-chuck'.

The species is confined to the Lesser Antilles where it occurs on Montserrat, Guadeloupe, Dominica and St Lucia. It is reasonably common on Montserrat but rare elsewhere. On Dominica, though widely distributed, it may have been affected by damage to canopy trees from recent hurricanes which has reduced the area of open leaf litter. A similar problem may face the species on Montserrat after hurricane Hugo. It is almost restricted to rain forest and although occurring from canopy to ground level, feeds often on the ground amongst leaf litter. The forest thrush feeds on insects and fruit, and builds a cup-shaped nest of moss fairly low down in a small tree, bush or tree fern. Two to three greenish-blue eggs are laid sometime between April and July.

MOCKINGBIRDS AND THRASHERS *Mimidae*

Tropical Mockingbird
LENGTH: 25 cm (10 in)

Mimus gilvus
LOCAL NAME: Grive Blanche

This species has a dark, slender, slightly curved bill, grey head and back, mainly dark wings and a long blackish tail with white tips to the outer tail feathers. The wing feathers are usually edged with white. The underparts are white or pale grey although this is buffish in immatures who also are browner above. At rest, mockingbirds often flick their long tail from side to side. They are very vocal with a musical series of notes, frequently repeated.

The tropical mockingbird occurs in the southern Lesser Antilles from Guadeloupe to Grenada (except Barbados), particularly in open lowland country and around human settlement in parks and gardens. It feeds largely on insects but also fruit. It builds a rough nest of twigs in a bush or tree, laying 3 – 4 green spotted eggs between March and July.

Northern Mockingbird   *Mimus polyglottos*
LENGTH: 25 cm (10 in)   LOCAL NAMES: Ruiseñor, Rossignol

A North American species, the northern mockingbird also breeds in the Greater Antilles including the US Virgin Islands (St Thomas and St Croix). It is very similar to the previous species but with much more white on the wings and tail. Its song is also more melodious and it sometimes mimics other species. The call note is a harsh, scolding 'check'. Its feeding and nesting habits are also similar with 3 – 4 bluish-green eggs laid in an open nest, mainly between January and July.

White-breasted Thrasher *Ramphocinclus brachyurus*
LENGTH: 23 – 24 cm (9 – 9½ in) LOCAL NAME: Gorge-blanc

A rather smart looking thrasher, this species has dark sooty brown upperparts becoming blackish on the sides of the head, and contrasting white underparts (from the chin down to the belly). The flanks of Martinique birds are also pale, contrasting with the back. It has a reddish eye and a slender, slightly curved bill. It commonly flicks its wings, particularly when a threat arises. The song is a soft mewing and the alarm call is a sharp 'tick', and a low hissing call.

The white-breasted thrasher occurs only on the Lesser Antillean islands of Martinique and St Lucia. The Martinique population (numbering around 40 pairs) is restricted to dry scrub woodland on the Caravelle peninsula in the north of the island, whilst on St Lucia an estimated population of around 60 pairs is confined to riverine dry forest in a handful of valleys on the north-east coast between Petite Anse and Dennery Knob just south of Louvet (particularly in Ravine la Chaloupe). The main threat to this species is habitat loss for charcoal production and the planting of cassava (and illegal marijuana).

The species is largely ground-dwelling, feeding on insects in the leaf litter although it will also take berries. It builds a bulky deep cup-shaped nest in saplings or shrubs at around 2 – 5 metres height, laying 2 – 3 pale blue eggs mainly between April and July.

White-breasted Thrasher

Scaly-breasted Thrasher

Scaly-breasted Thrasher
LENGTH: 22 cm (9 in)

Margarops fuscus
LOCAL NAME: Grive

The scaly-breasted thrasher is a thrush-like bird, dark greyish-brown above and white below though this is partially concealed by heavy markings of grey-brown. It has a short slender black bill with a slightly hooked tip. The outer tail feathers are conspicuously tipped with white and there is a white stripe on the wings which shows in flight. The eye is yellow in adults and brown in immatures. Its song is a quiet musical jumble of notes and alarm call is a short harsh 'chek-chek'.

This species occurs only in the Lesser Antilles, where it is found on Saba, St Eustatius, and the islands from Barbuda and Antigua south to Grenada (though rare in Barbados and possibly now extinct from Grenada). It is a shy species and prefers the canopy of trees or tall shrubs although it will also feed on the ground, for example upon rotting bananas. It is relatively common on most of the islands, occurring particularly in lowland dry woodland but also in rain forest. It feeds mainly on fruits from a wide variety of trees and shrubs, but also upon insects. The species builds a cup-shaped nest of twigs often high up in the fork of a tree, laying 2 – 3 greenish-blue eggs sometime between March and July.

Pearly-eyed Thrasher
LENGTH: 28 – 30 cm (11 – 12 in)

Margarops fuscatus
LOCAL NAMES: Grosse Grive, Paw-paw Bird

This species broadly resembles the scaly-breasted thrasher but is bigger, with a much larger pinkish or brownish-yellow hooked bill. The upperparts are paler grey-brown except for the wings which are darker tinged with brown. The whitish eye contrasting with the black pupil is also distinctive when viewed close-up. Like the previous species, it has conspicuous white tips to the outer tail feathers. Its song is a hesitant 'pio-tereu-tsee', rather louder and purer than the scaly-breasted thrasher and with quite long pauses between the phrases. It has a shrill note of alarm and a harsh 'chook', somewhat similar to its smaller relative.

The pearly-eyed thrasher is found throughout the Eastern Caribbean except the southernmost Lesser Antilles (Barbados, St Vincent, the Grenadines and Grenada). It occurs primarily in rain forest though is also found in secondary wooded vegetation and adjacent tree plantations. Less arboreal than the previous species, it feeds not only in the canopy but often also on the ground or in the understorey. Although feeding on fruits from a variety of tree and shrub species, insects may figure more highly in its diet than for the scaly-breasted thrasher. The species competes for nest cavities with other birds. It is aggressive and may eat the eggs and young of various species including parrots, to which it has been a threat. It nests in tree cavities, on the side of a cliff or cave, or in a tree or bush where it builds a bulky cup-shaped nest. Two to three greenish-blue eggs are laid mainly between March and July, although nesting may take place in most months of the year.

Trembler
LENGTH: 22 – 25 cm (9 – 10 in)

Cinclocerthia ruficauda
LOCAL NAME: Trembleur

A very distinctive thrasher, the trembler has a long, slender curved bill, brown to olive-grey upperparts and pale grey to white underparts. Its name comes from the habit it has of trembling the wings. The eyes are bright orange-yellow in adults and brown in immatures. The bill is much longer in the female than the male. Both the wing primaries and outer tail feathers may be rufous

Pearly-eyed Thrasher

Trembler

edged. Birds from Martinique and St Lucia are brownish-grey rather than reddish-brown, with less sexual size dimorphism. These differences may justify the separation of the two forms into separate species. The song is very quiet twittering, and the call a harsh 'chet-chet', rather similar to other thrashers.

The trembler is confined to the Lesser Antilles where it occurs on Saba, St Eustatius, St Kitts, Nevis, Montserrat, Guadeloupe, Dominica, Martinique (possibly extinct), St Lucia and St Vincent. It is found mainly in, or close to, rain forest. Though nowhere very common, it is easily overlooked, being a generally silent, inconspicuous species mainly of the understorey. It has a broad diet including a variety of insects and small berries, tree frogs and small lizards. The nest is commonly built in a tree cavity, although it may also be placed at the base of a palm frond or within a bromeliad in the fork of a tree. Two to three greenish-blue eggs are laid usually between March and August.

VIREOS   *Vireonidae*

Black-whiskered Vireo   *Vireo altiloquus*
LENGTH: 16 – 17 cm (6½ in)   LOCAL NAMES: Chouèque, Oiseau Canne, Père Gris, Julián Chiví, John-chew-it, John-to-whit

Vireos are small inconspicuous arboreal birds about the size and shape of a large warbler but less active and with a heavier bill. The black-whiskered vireo is the only representative of this family to be widespread in the Eastern Caribbean, occurring throughout the region though uncommon in the Virgin Islands, Saba and St Martin/Maarten. Juvenile birds in particular may migrate south to winter (September – February) in northern South America. The species has olive-green upperparts, paler sides to the face with a black stripe through the eye and white stripe above. The underparts are whitish with yellowish-green on the flanks. The black bill is relatively large, and the eye is reddish-brown in the adult and dull brown in immatures. The song is reminiscent of a Caribbean elaenia, though harsher and commonly of three syllables. There is also a sharp, nasal note and a thin, unmusical 'tsit'.

It occurs in most wooded habitats from sea level to mountain rain forest, although commonest in dry scrub woodland. It feeds on insects and fruit, and builds a pendant nest cup a few metres off the ground in a tree or shrub, laying 2 – 3 spotted white eggs between March and July.

Black-whiskered Vireo

WOOD WARBLERS   *Parulinae*

A wide range of North American wood warblers migrate through the Caribbean on their way to or from their wintering grounds in South America. Some remain in the West Indies through the winter. Although the Greater Antilles receives larger numbers and a greater variety of species, several species do also visit the Lesser Antilles. Those detailed below are the more common representatives of this family in the Eastern Caribbean. However, as was recommended for waders, the visitor is advised to expect sightings of other species (see Check-list) and to consult one of the North American identification guides. Details are given of the songs of different species, but generally they are silent when in those islands except for quiet 'chips'. Usually if a song is uttered it is in spring and rarely a full rendering.

Northern Parula Warbler
LENGTH: 10 – 12 cm (4 – 5 in)

Parula americana
LOCAL NAME: Reinita pechidorado

This species is a regular and fairly common passage migrant and winter visitor to the Eastern Caribbean, though rare in the southern Lesser Antilles south of Dominica. In winter, the parula warbler has olive-green upperparts which become greyish-blue in breeding plumage except for the mantle of the back which remains olive-green. There are two broad white bars on the wings and some white in the outer tail feathers. The throat is yellow and the rest of the underparts white except for males in breeding plumage which have a well-defined black and chestnut band just below the throat. Its song is a rising buzzy trill, dropping abruptly at the end, and the call is a sweet 'toip'.

Yellow Warbler
LENGTH: 12 – 14 cm (5 – 5½ in)

Dendroica petechia
LOCAL NAMES: Canary, Canario de Mangle, Mangrove Canary, Yellow Bird, Titine

The only widespread breeding warbler in the Eastern Caribbean, the yellow warbler occurs throughout the region except for Saba and the far southern Lesser Antilles (St Vincent, most of the Grenadines, and Grenada) where it is visited only in winter by North·American migrants. As suggested by the name, this species is brightly coloured yellow. The male is brighter than the female with greenish yellow upperparts and the head colour varying from a dark chestnut (Barbados) or pale chestnut cap (St Lucia, Dominica to the Virgin Islands) to a chestnut head (Martinique). The underparts are golden yellow streaked with chestnut. Females are greener above with plain yellow underparts. Juveniles have whitish underparts. The song is very variable between islands, but is a musical 'wee-chee-wee-chee-chee-wur'. Its call is a repeated 'chip', and a thin 'zeet'.

The species is common in lowland dry scrub woodland and coastal mangrove swamp, although it will occasionally follow cultivation into mountainous areas. Like other wood warblers, it is primarily insectivorous although it will take small berries. It builds a neat cup-shaped nest often low down in a bush or low tree, and lays 2 – 3 spotted, greenish-white eggs mainly between February and June.

Yellow Warbler

Adelaide's Warbler

Plumbeous Warbler

Adelaide's Warbler
LENGTH: 12 – 13 cm (5 in)

Dendroica adelaidae
LOCAL NAMES: Reinita Mariposera, Christmas Bird, Petit Chitte

The Adelaide's warbler is grey, or brownish-grey (Barbuda) above, with a yellow streak above the eye, some yellow below the eye, and yellow underparts. There are two white bars on the wing and some white also in the tail. Its song is a variable trill and the call is a 'chick'. The species is confined to the islands of Puerto Rico, Vieques, Barbuda and St Lucia where it occurs mainly in lowland forest and dry scrub although on St Lucia it extends into mountain rain forest. Its cup-shaped nest is built 1 to 2.5 metres above ground in a thick shrub or tree, into which 2 – 3 spotted white eggs are laid, mainly between March and July.

Plumbeous Warbler
LENGTH: 14 cm (5½ in)

Dendroica plumbea
LOCAL NAMES: Papia, Tic-tic

A very confiding warbler, this species is common in understorey vegetation of dry scrub woodland, rain forest and elfin woodland in Guadeloupe (including Marie-Galante and Terre-de-haut) and Dominica. The adult has slate-grey upperparts, a white eye-stripe, and two white wing-bars. The underparts are greyish-white. Immatures are olive green above, also with two white wing-bars, but a grey tail. The eye-stripe is yellowish as are the underparts. The song is a short melodious 'pa-pi-a', and calls include a loud rattle and a short 'chek'. It feeds upon insects which it gleans from leaves, and small berries. The nest is a small cup built low down often in a bush or bromeliad clump, and 2 – 3 spotted eggs are laid between March and July.

Whistling Warbler
LENGTH: 14 cm (5½ in)

Catharopeza bishopi
LOCAL NAME: Whistling Bird

This blackish warbler is confined to mountain forest and elfin woodland (for example Richmond Peak, and the Colonarie and Perseverence valleys) on St Vincent. It has blackish upperparts with a white eye-ring and spot at the base of the bill. The underparts are white becoming greyer on the flanks and with a black throat beneath which is a white then black band across the upper breast. Immatures are brownish, paler on the underparts but with a darkish band across the upper breast. The song is a rising series of short, rich notes, terminating with two or three emphatic notes. The call is a short 'tuk'. It feeds on the ground in the shrub layer and understorey, mainly on insects. The cup-shaped nest is built low down in a tree or shrub, with two spotted eggs laid probably mainly between April and July.

Semper's Warbler
LENGTH: 14 cm (5½ in)

Leucopeza semperi
LOCAL NAME: Pied-blanc

The Semper's warbler is restricted to the understorey of mountain forest and elfin woodland (around Piton Flore) on St Lucia. However, despite searches, it has not been seen since 1972, and sadly may now be extinct. A rather plain warbler, this species had dark grey upperparts and whitish underparts. Immatures have olive-green upperparts (particularly the rump and uppertail coverts) and brownish-buff underparts. Its breeding habits are not known.

Black-and-white Warbler
LENGTH: 13 – 14 cm (5 – 5½ in)

Mniotilta varia
LOCAL NAMES: Reinita trepadora,
Mi-Deuil

A very distinctive warbler, this species has longitudinal black and white stripes down its body, with black more prevalent on the back and white on the underparts. The black stripes are broader on the

Black-and-white Warbler

head, typically giving rise to a black crown and cheeks interspersed with white. Females are duller than males, and the streaks on the underparts are less distinct. It has the characteristic habit of creeping along branches and around the trunks of trees, and is best seen in citrus orchards or woodland edge. The song, a high thin whistle, may sometimes be heard on migration. The species is a regular passage migrant and winter visitor (September – April) throughout the Eastern Caribbean, though commonest in the Greater Antilles.

Yellow-rumped or Myrtle Warbler — *Dendroica coronata*
LENGTH: 14 cm (5½ in)   LOCAL NAME: Reinita coronada

Another distinctive warbler, this species has a grey or greyish-brown back streaked with black, white throat and underparts with some black on the breast, two white wing bars and some white in the tail. There are also conspicuous yellow patches on the crown, sides of the breast and rump, although immature females have yellow only on the rump, the rest of the body being dull brown streaked with black. Adult females, and males in winter plumage are also duller brown than summer males. The song is a soft warble and the call a hard 'check'. It is an uncommon passage migrant and winter visitor (November – April) to the Eastern Caribbean, wintering mainly in the Greater Antilles, though also occurring as an irregular passage migrant in the more northerly Lesser Antilles, where it may be seen feeding in coastal dry scrub mainly in spring.

In autumn and winter, the species may be confused with the **Cape May Warbler** *Dendroica tigrina*, an uncommon but regular winter visitor to the Eastern Caribbean. The latter is best distinguished by some yellow behind the ear and on its striped breast, the yellowish brown rather than white throat, and the duller yellowish-green rump.

Blackpoll Warbler — *Dendroica striata*
LENGTH: 12 – 14 cm (5 – 5½ in)   LOCAL NAME: Reinita rayada

This North American warbler occurs in lowland dry woodland or tree plantations throughout the Eastern Caribbean where it occurs as an uncommon passage migrant (mainly in September – November) wintering in northern South America. In the Caribbean, most individuals are in winter plumage, being dull green above,

118

Blackpoll Warbler **Prothonotary Warbler**

with some black streaking on the mantle, and yellowish under-parts. The legs are pale yellow in colour. There are two white bars on each wing and some white in the tail. Males in spring develop a black crown with white sides to the head, white cheeks and white throat. The rest of the upperparts are olive-grey and the underparts white, both with fairly strong black streaking. Females in breeding plumage are duller with more greyish-green upperparts, whitish underparts, both streaked with black, but no white on the cheeks. Its song is a series of high, thin notes, delivered in a monotone, sometimes becoming louder in the middle of the song.

Prothonotary Warbler *Protonotaria citrea*
LENGTH: 14 cm (5½ in) LOCAL NAME: Reinita anaranjada

The prothonotary warbler is another regular though relatively uncommon passage migrant and winter visitor over a large part of the Eastern Caribbean. It is often found in the vicinity of mangrove swamps. The male has a bright orange-yellow head and underparts, a yellowish-green mantle and mainly blue-grey wings,

119

rump and uppertail coverts. The undertail coverts are white with much white in the tail. Females are duller with more uniform yellowish green upperparts and much less white on the tail. The song is loud and clear – an ascending series of rather slurred notes.

American Redstart
LENGTH: 13 cm (5 in)

Setophaga ruticilla

LOCAL NAMES: Petit du Feu, Gabriel du Feu, Christmas Bird, Candelita

This very active warbler may be seen throughout the Eastern Caribbean in dry forest understorey, often beside swampland. It is a regular passage migrant and winter visitor (mainly September – April) from North America, occurring most commonly in the Greater Antilles. The male is glossy black with a white belly and prominent orange patches on the wings and bases to the outer tail feathers. The female is olive-brown above, whitish below, with yellow rather than orange wing and tail patches. There may also be some yellow on the sides of the breast. Immature males may resemble females.

The species frequently droops its wings or fans its tail to reveal the orange or yellow patches, and flits out into the air after insects. It will also sometimes feed upon small berries. Its song is a series of similar high notes, sometimes with a sharp descent at the end, and the call is a sharp 'tschip'.

Ovenbird
LENGTH: 15 cm (6 in)

Seiurus aurocapillus

LOCAL NAME: Pizpita dorada

This North American warbler has plain olive-green upperparts, throat and breast heavily streaked with black, and the rest of the underparts are white. The centre of the crown is brownish-orange in the adult, duller in immatures, with a black stripe on either side. There is also a distinctive white ring around the eye with some white near the base of the bill. It occurs in the Caribbean as a regular passage migrant and winter visitor (September – April), though relatively uncommon in the Virgin Islands (besides St John where it is more common) and the Lesser Antilles. It is a ground-walking species of dry woodland, shrubbery and swamp edge. In spring it sings from an exposed perch in the understorey, making a loud and clear 'tea-cher' repeated around ten times.

120

American Redstart

Northern Waterthrush

Northern Waterthrush   *Seiurus noveboracensis*
LENGTH: 13 – 15 in (5 – 6 in)   LOCAL NAME: Pizpita de Mangle

Resembling the previous species, the northern waterthrush has plain dark olive-brown upperparts, and pale buffish-yellow underparts streaked with black. It is best distinguished by its yellowish or cream stripe above the eye and the lack of a white eye-ring. A close relative, the **Louisiana waterthrush** *Seiurus motacilla*, which only rarely occurs in the region, has a larger bill and a pure unstreaked throat. Both species typically bob their tail.

The northern waterthrush is a regular passage migrant and winter visitor throughout the Eastern Caribbean (September – April), commonest in the Greater Antilles. It is another ground dwelling warbler, found particularly on the edge of swamp or lake vegetation, where it takes insects, molluscs and small crabs. It has a loud and ringing 'tchip', and a metallic 'chink' call, and can be attracted by making a swishing sound.

BANANAQUITS (HONEYCREEPERS)   *Coerebinae*

Bananaquit   *Coereba flaveola*
LENGTH: 10 – 13 cm (4 – 5 in)   LOCAL NAMES: Sucrier, Reinita, Sugar Bird, Yellow-breast

One of the most common and widely distributed birds in the Caribbean, the bananaquit occurs throughout the region, and though most abundant in secondary vegetation, plantations and gardens, it may be found in virtually any habitat. Like other honeycreepers, the bananaquit has a short, slender curved bill. It is a colourful small bird, with sooty grey or black upperparts, a yellow or greenish-yellow rump, and yellow breast and belly. There is a conspicuous stripe above the eye which is white in adults and yellow in juveniles. In some populations, a conspicuous white spot also shows on the wings. It is a noisy bird, with a short ticking alarm note, and a frequently repeated wheezy song 'zee-e-e-e-swees-te'.

There is much plumage colour variation between the islands. In the southernmost Lesser Antilles (Grenada and St Vincent), most individuals are black except for a slightly greenish-yellow wash on the breast and uppertail coverts. Further north, the extent of black diminishes so that birds in Dominica, for example, have a conspicuous yellow breast and belly, although retaining a sooty

122

Bananaquit

grey throat and head (except for the eye-stripe). Birds from the northern Antilles may have a greyish-white throat.

The species feeds not only upon nectar, but also the juices of various fruits (including cultivated plants such as banana, mango, citrus, and pawpaw), seeds of herbaceous plants, and a variety of small insects. Although breeding mainly takes place between March and August, there is no distinct season and nests may be found in any month of the year. As the season progresses, males show a greater tendency to mate with a second female, leaving their first partner to care for the brood. The nest is a round mass of leaves and grass fibres with a small hole in the side, into which 2 – 3 heavily spotted, whitish eggs are laid. It is usually placed in a bush or near the end of a branch at a height of several metres. More roughly built nests may be used as a night roost.

TANAGERS   *Thraupinae*

Antillean or Blue-hooded Euphonia   *Euphonia musica*
LENGTH: 11 – 12 cm (4½ – 5 in)   LOCAL NAMES: Mistletoe Bird, Christmas Bird, Canario del País

In the Eastern Caribbean, this beautiful little tanager is found on most of the Lesser Antilles (Saba, St Bartholemew, Barbuda, Antigua, Montserrat, Guadeloupe, Dominica, Martinique, St Lucia, St Vincent, Bequia and Grenada, though possibly no longer a regular breeder from the last). It is generally uncommon (particularly in the more southerly islands) and though usually occurring in small groups, its presence is probably often overlooked. It is more readily heard than seen, uttering a soft twittering song from the tree canopy. It makes a variety of distinctive call notes including a rapid, gentle, almost tinkling 'ti-tit' and a hard, metallic 'chi-chink'. A small bird, the euphonia has a short finch-like bill and short tail. It has a pale blue crown extending as a narrow line to the side of the neck, a yellow forehead (with a narrow black posterior border) and chin, yellowish-green back and underparts becoming yellowish on the rump. There is some plumage variation between island groups. Although the sexes are similar in the Lesser Antilles, males from Puerto Rico differ in having a violet blue crown extending down the back and wings to the tail, excepting the yellow rump. The underparts are also yellow.

Blue-hooded Euphonia

The species occurs particularly in mountain rain forest although it may also be found in both lowland dry woodland and secondary scrub. It is a very mobile species, its movements apparently determined by the presence of fruiting mistletoe, its favoured food. There may be seasonal movements into lowland areas where it is often seen in cultivated areas and gardens in midwinter, hence its local name 'Christmas Bird'. Breeding occurs between April (sometimes early as January) and July with four spotted eggs laid in a globular nest built among vines or in a tall tree.

Lesser Antillean or Hooded Tanager   *Tangara cucullata*
LENGTH: 15 cm (6 in)   LOCAL NAMES: Prince Bird, Dos-bleu

The Lesser Antillean tanager occurs only on St Vincent and Grenada where it is common at all levels in wooded cultivation, dry scrub woodland, and rain forest even to montane thicket and palm brake. It has a chestnut crown, blackish sides to the head, a pale metallic-gold back, and bluish-green wings and tail. The underparts are buffish with a violet-blue wash. Females are duller than males, with a greenish back, wings and tail. The crown varies in colour from a rich reddish-chestnut in the St Vincent population to dark chestnut in Grenada birds. The call is a weak 'weet-weet-weet-witwitwitwit'. Like other tanagers, it feeds almost entirely on fruit. It builds a cup-shaped nest in a bush or low tree, laying two spotted eggs between April and July.

BLACKBIRDS AND ALLIES   *Icterinae*

Carib Grackle   *Quiscalus lugubris*
LENGTH: 24 – 27 cm (9½ – 11 in)   LOCAL NAMES: Merle, Blackbird, Bequia-sweet

The carib grackle is found throughout the Lesser Antilles from St Martin south to Grenada, including Barbados. It has also been introduced to Barbuda, Antigua, St Kitts, and St Martin. It is commonest on those islands with extensive areas of open lowland country and settlement, and in these regions may be seen in active flocks.

The male is black glossed with purple, with a conspicuous yellow eye. The female is much smaller and duller, although its plumage varies between islands. It ranges from dull black on Barbados, brownish-black from Grenada to St Lucia, and pale brown with whitish throat and underparts from Montserrat to Martinique. The immature is brownish-black with brown eyes. Grackles have a pointed heavy black bill, long keel-shaped tail, and relatively long legs which enable them to run about grassland looking for insects. They will also sometimes take seeds, and readily feed upon scraps. The species roosts and nests colonially, building large cup-shaped nests often high above the ground in a tall palm or other tree, and laying 2 – 4 bluish, spotted eggs. It has an extended breeding season, nesting in most months of the year, though possibly mainly between February and July. It is a noisy species, making various harsh clucks and squeaks, with a ringing bell-like finale. Common sounds have been rendered as a squeaky 'etsywee', and a musical 'wee-tsi-ke-tsi-ke-tsi-ke'. These notes are very variable between islands.

Carib Grackle

Shiny Cowbird

Shiny or Glossy Cowbird
LENGTH: 18 – 20 cm (7 – 8 in)

Molothrus bonariensis
LOCAL NAMES: Merle de Sainte Lucie, Merle de Barbade, Corn Bird, Tordo, Blackbird's Cousin

The shiny cowbird is a South American species which has recently colonised the Lesser Antilles north to Martinique (also recorded on Antigua and Marie-Galante), and the Greater Antilles as far east as the Virgin Islands (St John, St Thomas, and Tortola). It is a bird of lowland open country, often close to human settlement. The species is gregarious and may roost colonially, associating with grackles. The male is black, glossed with purple; the female duller brown, darker on the wings and tail, light brownish-grey on the underparts with a light stripe above the eye. Immatures are similar to adult females but with a yellowish streak above the eye and underparts buffish. Though resembling grackles, it is distinguished by its brown eyes, short, dark bill and shorter, often upturned, tail. The song is a series of loud, musical whistles interspersed with melodious warbles; also a soft unmusical 'ka-wuk' (with rising second syllable).

This species is omnivorous, feeding on insects as well as grain and other seeds. It is parasitic, depositing its eggs sometime between December and July in the nests of other birds such as orioles and grackles, although many species are vulnerable. Several females may lay in the same nest, and, like cuckoos, usually the young of the host are unable to compete with the intruder.

St Lucia Oriole
LENGTH: 20 – 21 cm (8 – 8½ in)

Icterus laudabilis
LOCAL NAME: Carouge

An island endemic, this oriole is confined to St Lucia where it has a wide distribution from coastal vegetation and dry scrub to tree plantations and rain forest. Although not uncommon, it faces a potential threat from glossy cowbirds which arrived in 1931 and may frequently parasitise the nests of orioles.

Its plumage is mainly black but with bright orange or orange-yellow patches on the upper and underwing coverts. The female has the orange patches paler and more yellow. Immatures are mainly greenish. Like other orioles, the song is a series of loud melodious whistles, though more protracted and musical. It feeds upon insects as well as a variety of fruit. The nest is a fairly strong structure, basket-shaped and suspended from the leaf of a tree, usually 2 – 4 m from the ground. Two to three spotted eggs are laid sometime between April and July.

Montserrat Oriole
LENGTH: 20 – 21 cm (8 – 8½ in)

Icterus oberi

LOCAL NAMES: Tannia Bird,
Blantyre Bird

As its name implies, this oriole is confined to the island of Montserrat where it is found in rain forest particularly above 800 m in the Soufriere Hills and centre of the island (Chance Peak, bamboo forest above Galway's Soufriere on the footpath to Roche's Estate, and at Olveston tapped spring on Runaway Ghaut). The total population is estimated to number only 1200 birds, and possibly less, and the species faces threats from further habitat destruction.

Like other orioles, the male is mainly black but with yellow patches on the upper and underwing coverts, bend of the wing and rump, and yellowish-orange on the uppertail coverts, belly and undertail coverts. The female (and immature) differs in having yellowish olive-green upperparts and golden-yellow underparts. Its song is a series of loud and melodious whistles, and the call is a sharp 'chic'. It has a diet almost exclusively of insects, and builds a basket-shaped nest suspended from a banana, bread-fruit, palm or other forest tree. Two to three spotted eggs are laid sometime between April and July.

Martinique Oriole
LENGTH: 20 cm (8 in)

Icterus bonana

LOCAL NAME: Carouge

The only bird species confined to Martinique is this oriole which occurs in all forest types from lowland dry scrub, wooded gardens, and tree plantations to rain forest up to 550 m. Although widespread, it is not common and is thought to be declining in the face of brood parasitism from the now abundant glossy cowbird (which was first recorded in 1948) and nest predation by the Carib grackle. This species has less black on it than some other orioles. The head, neck and upper breast are dark chestnut. The mantle, tail and most of the wings are black; there are tawny patches on the upperwing coverts and belly, and orange-red on the rump. The song is a series of loud melodious whistles. Feeding and nesting habits are similar to the St Lucia oriole although breeding usually begins in February and the nest may be built at a height of 10 m above the ground.

Troupial *Icterus icterus*
LENGTH: 25 – 28 cm (10 – 11 in) LOCAL NAME: Turpial

This large oriole has been introduced to St Thomas (south and east coasts) and Water Island in the Virgin Islands (and to Puerto Rico) where it is now established. Elsewhere, it occurs as an irregular transient visitor to the Lesser Antilles. The species has a black head, throat, mantle, wings and tail but with extensive white on the wings. The rest of the back and rump is orange-yellow, and there is a broad orange-yellow collar across the nape of the neck, extending down over the breast and belly. The iris is conspicuously white (in the other orioles it is dark brown or black) and this is surrounded by blue or bluish bare skin. The song is a variety of loud whistles 'troup, troup, troup', or 'troup-ial, troup-ial, troup-ial'. The species build a deep purse-shaped nest, suspended from a tree or thorny scrub, into which are laid 3 – 4 spotted eggs.

CARDINALS, GROSBEAKS, AND ALLIES *Cardinalinae*

Streaked Saltator *Saltator albicollis*
LENGTH: 20 – 22 cm (8 – 8½ in) LOCAL NAMES: Gros-bec, Grive
Gros-bec

The streaked saltator, found in large parts of Central and South America, occurs in the Eastern Caribbean only on the Lesser Antillean islands of Guadeloupe, Dominica, Martinique and St Lucia. This species is a large finch with a powerful broad yellow and black bill which it uses for feeding upon a wide range of fruits and large seeds. It has dull yellowish-green upperparts becoming brown on the wing primaries and tail, and a yellowish-white stripe above the eye. The underparts are white streaked with olive-green except on the throat which is fringed black. It is a retiring species of thick undergrowth, scrub and secondary vegetation, particularly in lowland dry areas. It is more often heard than seen, the song being a very distinctive and far-carrying series of musical notes, first ascending and then descending. Breeding takes place mainly between April and July, with a cup-shaped nest built in a bush or low tree and 2 – 3 eggs laid. The eggs are light greenish-blue with black scrawls at either end.

Streaked Saltator

Male Black-faced Grassquit

Female Black-faced Grassquit

Black-faced Grassquit *Tiaris bicolor*
LENGTH: 11 – 12 cm (4½ in)   LOCAL NAMES: Si-si-zeb, Gorrión Negro, Chipsa, Sinbird, Grass Sparrow, Tobacco Bird

An abundant and widely distributed small finch, the black-faced grassquit is found throughout the Eastern Caribbean. It is an open country species of grassland, scrub, thicket and garden, particularly to be seen in waste ground along the roadside or field margins. It feeds predominantly upon the seeds of herbs and grasses which in the Greater Antilles it takes more often from the ground than the previous species. The male has dark green upperparts with extensive black over the head, and underparts extending over the breast becoming greyish on the belly. The female is very similar to the female **yellow-faced grassquit** *Tiaris olivacea* (of most of the Greater Antilles including Vieques and Culebra but not the main Virgin Islands), being overall greyish-green above with paler greyish underparts, although it entirely lacks yellow on the head. The local name in the Lesser Antilles describes its characteristic song, a buzzing 'si-si-zeb' but with many variations. The call is a soft, musical 'tsip'. The nest is placed in a tree or bush, rarely on the ground as in the yellow-faced grassquit. Like other small finches, the nest is round, composed of grasses and other herbs with a side entrance, in which 2 – 4 spotted, whitish eggs are laid. Breeding may take place in virtually any month of the year, though primarily between March and August.

Blue-black Grassquit or *Volatinia jacarina*
Blue-black Seedeater
LENGTH: 10 – 12 cm (4 – 4½ in)   LOCAL NAMES: Blue-black Si-si, Si-si-zeb Noir, Prézite

A small South American grassquit, this species has been established in the Lesser Antilles on Grenada at least since the beginning of this century and is now rather common. It also occurs in Trinidad and Tobago. It is a small compact bird with a short stubby black bill. The male is glossy blue-black all over. The female is dull olive-brown above and has paler brown underparts with heavy blackish streaking. The immature male resembles the female but is more blackish. The song is a wheezy 'jwee', uttered by the male in the course of a characteristic short upward leap from a post or other perch, with wings and tail outspread.

This species is usually seen in lowland open scrub woodland, beside fields and rough ground where it feeds mainly upon grass seeds. In Grenada it is common only in the semi-arid south-west. The nest is a small cup of grass placed in a grass clump or low in a bush. Two pale greenish-blue spotted eggs are laid usually between March and August.

Yellow-bellied Seedeater
Sporophila nigricollis
LENGTH: 12 cm (4½ in)   LOCAL NAME: White-beak Si-si

This South American finch occurs in the Eastern Caribbean only on Grenada and neighbouring Carriacou (also Trinidad and Tobago). It is found in lowland scrub woodland and grassland although it will also occur at midlevels in secondary vegetation. The male has a black head and throat, the rest of the upperparts being olive-green and underparts yellow or yellowish-white. The female has plain greenish-brown upperparts and buffish underparts becoming more yellowish or white on the belly. The presence of yellow on the underparts of birds of either sex helps to distinguish it from the previous species. The song is a short melodious warble. Its diet is mainly grass seeds, as indicated by its name. The nest is a small cup situated in a bush or low tree, into which 2 – 3 spotted eggs are laid mainly between March and August.

Lesser Antillean Bullfinch
Loxigilla noctis
LENGTH: 14 – 15 cm (5½ – 6 in)   LOCAL NAMES: Père Noir (male), Moisson (female), Robin, Sparrow, Red-breast, Rouge-gorge

This species is one of the commonest birds of the Lesser Antilles, occurring throughout these islands with the exception of the Grenadines. It also colonised St John in the Virgin Islands around 1960. The species may be found at all elevations from sea-level to mountain top, and in all habitats though it is most numerous along the forest edge, in secondary vegetation, shrubbery and gardens. The male is glossy black but with red patches in front of the eye, on the chin and throat, and orange on the undertail coverts. It has a broad black bill. The female is brownish or olive-brown above with greyish underparts and orange undertail coverts, and a yellowish bill. Immatures resemble females but young males may show some black around the head and have a grey or blackish bill.

133

Male Lesser Antillean Bullfinch

In Barbados, males have a similar plumage to females. Bullfinches make a variety of sounds from a harsh 'chuck' and shrill 'tseep-tseep', to a sharp, short trill.

The species is omnivorous, feeding mainly on fruits and seeds but also upon insects. It will readily visit scraps of food provided by humans, and is attracted to ripe fallen fruit such as bananas, citrus or pawpaw. The breeding season is extended though mainly between February and August. A round nest with side entrance is built in a thick bush or tree, usually 3 – 5 metres from the ground, in which 2 – 3 spotted eggs are laid.

St Lucia Black Finch   *Melanospiza richardsoni*
LENGTH: 14 cm (5½ in)   LOCAL NAME: Moisson Pied-blanc

This species is confined to the island of St Lucia where though uncommon, it is widespread from dry coastal scrub to rain forest and tree plantations. It favours dense understorey and thick leaf litter where it feeds upon a variety of fruits and insects, close to or on the ground. The male is all-black except for its pale pink legs.

The female resembles that of the Lesser Antillean bullfinch (which is also present on St Lucia), but it has a grey crown contrasting with the brown back, and the underparts are buffish. The bill is also larger in this species, and the legs are pale pink. Immature males resemble females but are darker. Other useful identifying features are the more direct flight and the habit of flicking its tail. The song is a wheezy 'tic-zwee-swizewiz-you', reminiscent of a bananaquit. The nest is a bulky loose round nest with a side entrance, situated near the ground in a young tree or bamboo, in which two spotted eggs are laid, sometime between March and August.

Grassland Yellow Finch
LENGTH: 12 – 13 cm (4½ – 5 in)

Sicalis luteola
LOCAL NAMES: Grass Sparrow, Grass Canary, Petit Serin

This small South American finch was introduced to Barbados around 1900. Since then it has spread to St Lucia, Martinique and Guadeloupe. A small population also became established on St Vincent after a hurricane in 1971, but this now appears to be extinct. It is yellowish-green or brownish above, heavily streaked with blackish marks except on the rump and uppertail coverts. There are often two white wing bars. The face and underparts are bright yellow. Males are brighter than females, whilst immatures are paler yellow below with additional blackish streaking on the throat and breast. Its call, often uttered in flight, is a shrill but melodious series of short notes. The species occurs mainly in short grassland where it actively moves around in small flocks, feeding mainly upon seeds. The nest is cup-shaped, built on the ground, into which 2 – 3 spotted eggs are laid. The breeding season is extended, though mainly between March and August.

Bibliography

Babbs, S., Ling, S., Robertson, P. and Wood, P. (1987) *Report of the 1986 University of East Anglia Martinique Oriole Expedition*, ICBP Study Report No. 23. Cambridge.

Babbs, S., Buckton, S., Robertson, P. and Wood, P. (1988) *Report of the 1987 UEA/ICBP St Lucia Expedition*. ICBP Study Report No. 33. Cambridge.

Belbeoc'h, B. (1980) *L'avifaune de la mangrove de Guadeloupe*, Office National des Forets, Fort de France, Guadeloupe.

Benito-Espinal, E. (1991) *Birds of the French Antilles*. Paris, France.

Blockstein, D.E. (1991) Population declines of the endangered endemic birds on Grenada, West Indies. *Bird Conservation International* 1: 83 – 91.

Bond, J. (1979a) *Birds of the West Indies*, Collins, London.

Bond, J. (1979b) Derivations of Lesser Antillean Birds, *Proc. Acad. Nat. Sci. Phil.* 131: 89 – 103.

Butler, P. (1980) The St Lucia Amazon *(Amazona versicolor)*: its changing status and conservation, pp. 171 – 180 in R.F. Pasquier (editor) *Conservation of New World Parrots*, ICBP Techn. Publ. No. 1, Smithsonian Institution Press, Washington.

Diamond, A.W. (1973) Habitats and feeding stations of St Lucia forest birds, *Ibis* 115: 313 – 329.

Evans, P.G.H. (1986) Dominica multiple landuse project, *Ambio* 15 (2): 82 – 89.

Evans, P.G.H. (1988) *The conservation status of the Imperial and Red-necked Parrots on the island of Dominica, West Indies*, ICBP Study Report No. 27. Cambridge.

Evans, P.G.H. (1991) Status and conservation of Imperial and Red-necked Parrots *Amazona imperialis* and *A. arausiaca* on Dominica. *Bird Conservation International* 1: 11 – 32.

Faaborg, J.R. and Arendt, W. (1985) *Wildlife assessments in the Caribbean*, Institute of Tropical Forestry, Rio Pedras, Puerto Rico.

ffrench, R. (1986) *Birds of Trinidad and Tobago*, Macmillan Caribbean, London.

Gregoire, F.W. (1980) The dilemma of the *Amazona imperialis* and *Amazona arausiaca* parrots in Dominica following hurricane David in 1979, pp. 161 – 167 in R.F. Pasquier (editor) *Conservation of New World Parrots*, ICBP Techn. Publ. No. 1, Smithsonian Institution Press, Washington.

Halewyn, R. van and Norton, R.L. (1984) The status and conservation of seabirds in the Caribbean, pp. 169 – 222 in J.P. Croxall, P.G.H. Evans and R.W. Schreiber (eds), *Status and conservation of the world's seabirds*, ICBP Techn. Publ. No. 2. Cambridge.

Hilder, P. (1989) *The Birds of Nevis*. The Nevis Historical and Conservation Society, Nevis.

Holland, C.S. and Williams, J.M. (1978) Observations on the Birds of Antigua. *American Birds* 32: 1095 – 1105.

Johnson, T.H. (1988) *Biodiversity and Conservation in the Caribbean: Profiles of Selected Islands*, ICBP Monograph No. 1. Cambridge.

Kepler, C.B. and Kepler, A.K. (1978) The seabirds of Culebra and its adjacent Islands, Puerto Rico. *Living Bird* 16: 21 – 50.

Lack, D., Lack, E., Lack, P. and Lack. A. (1073) Birds on St Vincent, *Ibis* 115: 46 – 52.

Lack, D. and Lack, A. (1973) Birds on Grenada, *Ibis* 115: 53 – 59.

Lack, D. (1976) *Island Biology*, Blackwell, Oxford.

Lambert, F. (1983) Report on an expedition to survey the status of the St Vincent Parrot *Amazona guildingii*, ICBP Study Report No. 3. Cambridge.

Lambert, F. (1985) The St Vincent Parrot, an endangered Caribbean bird, *Oryx* 19: 34 – 37.

Nichols, T.D. (1980) St Vincent Amazon (*Amazona guildingii*): predators, clutch size, plumage polymorphism, effect of the volcanic eruption and population estimate, pp. 197 – 208 in R.F. Pasquier (ed.), *Conservation of New World Parrots*, ICBP Techn. Publ. No. 1, Smithsonian Institution Press, Washington.

Pinchon, P. (1976) *Fauna des Antilles Françaises – Les Oiseaux*, Office National des Forets, Fort de France, Guadeloupe.

Raffaelle, H.A. (1983) *A guide to the birds of Puerto Rico and the Virgin Islands*, Fondo Educativo Interamericano Incorporada, Puerto Rico.

Robbins, C.S., Bruun, B. and Zim, H.S. (1983) *Birds of North America*, Golden Press, New York.

Scott, D.A. and Carbonell, M. (1986) *A directory of Neotropical wetlands*, IUCN, Cambridge and IWRB, Slimbridge.

Siegel, A. (1983) *Birds of Montserrat*, Montserrat National Trust, Montserrat.

Spencer, W.H.F. (1981) *A Guide to the Birds of Antigua*, Benji's Printery, St John's, Antigua.

Wunderle, J.M. (1985) An ecological comparison of the avifaunas of Grenada and Tobago, West Indies, *Wilson Bull.* 97: 356 – 365.

Bird-watching sites in the Eastern Caribbean

Virgin Islands (St Thomas, St John, Anegada, Jost Van Dyke, Tortola and Virgin Gorda)

Wetlands: Mangrove Lagoon and Benner Bay, Perseverence Bay Pond, Vessup Bay Pond, and Magen's Bay Wetland (St Thomas); Mary Point Pond (St John); Flamingo Pond Bird Sanctuary, East End Pond (Anegada); western Beef Island, Josiah's Bay to Paraquita Lagoon (Tortola); East End Harbour (Jost Van Dyke); South Sound Mangroves (Virgin Gorda); Brandy Point Pond (Prickly Pear Cay).

Seabird colonies: Cayo Luis Peña Peninsula, Flamenco, offshore islets (Culebra); Buck Island, Cockroach, Saba, Flat, Dutchcap and Frenchcap Cays, Little Cap Cay, Dog Island, Shark Island (St Thomas); Anegada; Tobago Island (west of Jost Van Dyke); George Dog (west of Virgin Gorda).

St Croix

Wetlands: Salt River Bay, Altona Lagoon, Southgate Pond, Coakley Bay Pond, Great Pond, Cassava Garden, Krause Lagoon, Manning Bay, and Vessup Bay Pond.

Seabird colonies: Cassava Garden, Buck Island.

Saba and St Eustatius

Seabird colonies: Green Island (noddy terns) and Diamond Rock (bridled terns, brown boobies), Saba; coast of St Eustatius, particularly White Wall on southern slope of The Quill (tropicbirds).

Sombrero, Anguilla, St Martin/St Maarten and St Barthelemy

Wetlands: Scrub Island, Savannah Pond, Cauls Pond, Long Salt Pond, Road Salt Pond, Rendezvous Pond, Meads Bay Pond, Cove Pond, West End Salt Pond, and Dog Island (Anguilla); Grand Etang de Simsonbaai, Etangs de Grand Case, Etang Chevrise and Cul-de-Sac, and Etang aux Poissons (St Martin); Great Salt Pond, Freshpond, Little Bay Pond (St Maarten); Grande Saline, Etang du Grand Cul-de-Sac, Etang de Toiny, Etang de St John, Etang de Public, and Anse de Marigot (St Barthelemy).

Seabird colonies: Sombrero; islets off Dog Island (Anguilla); Pelican Key and other cays off the east coast of St Martin/St Maarten.

St Kitts – Nevis

Wetlands: Greatheeds Pond, Half Moon Pond, Muddy Pond, Great Salt Pond (St Kitts); The Bogs, near Charleston; Nelson Spring; behind Hurricane Hill beach; near Nisbert Hotel; and behind beach at White Bay (Nevis).

Seabird Colonies: Greatheeds Pond (St Kitts).

Antigua and Barbuda

Wetlands: Salt Ponds on west coast, Parham Harbour and Guiana Bay, Five Island Harbour (Antigua); Codrington Lagoon, Bull Hole and inland mangroves (Barbuda).
Seabird colonies: Islands in Guiana Bay (for example Great Bird Island) and Mercer's Creek Bay (Antigua); Codrington Lagoon (Barbuda).

Montserrat and Redonda

Wetlands: Fox's Bay Bird Sanctuary, Belham River Estuary.
Seabird colonies: between Lime Kiln Bay and Rendezvous Bay (Montserrat); Redonda.
Endemic birds: montane forest of the Centre and Soufriere Hills above 800 m (Montserrat oriole).

Guadeloupe and Marie-Galante

Wetlands: Grand Cul-de-Sac Marin, Pointe d'Antigues Marsh, Moule Mangroves, Pointe des Chateaux Lagoons (Guadeloupe); Marais de Folle Anse (Marie-Galante).
Seabird colonies: Marie-Galante, Isles des Saintes.
Endemic birds: mainly rain forest up to 700 m on eastern slopes of Basse Terre (Guadeloupe woodpecker).

Dominica

Wetlands: Cabrits and Glanvillea swamps, Canefield pool, Melville Hall Flats.
Seabird colonies: Pointe de Fou; Mastle rock; Pointe Michel, Tarou cliffs, Pointe Coubari and Toucari (tropicbirds only).
Endemic birds: rain forest on slopes of Morne Diablotin (Imperial and red-necked parrots).

Martinique

Wetlands: Baie de Fort-de-France, Marais de Sainte Anne, Etang des Salines, Baie des Anglais.
Seabird colonies: Poirier islet in Baie des Anglais Daimant Rock.
Endemic birds: lowland scrub and rain forest to 500 m (Martinique Oriole).

St Lucia

Wetlands: Boid d'Orange Swamp, Marigot Bay, Savannes Bay (particularly Eau Piquant lagoon) and Boriel's Pond.
Seabird colonies: Maria Island north end of Anse la Chaloupe.
Endemic birds: montane forest of central region (St Lucia Parrot); rain forest around Piton Flore (Semper's Warbler; may now be extinct); all habitats (St Lucia Black Finch, St Lucia Oriole).

St Vincent and Grenadines

Wetlands: Milligan Cay, Sharp's Bay, Nilikin's Bay (St Vincent); Carriacou mangroves, Saline Island pond (Grenadines).
Seabird colonies: Milligan Cay and cliffs near Chateaubelair (St Vincent);

Hog Island in Woburn Bay, north coast of Bequia, and Battowia (Grenadines). *Endemic birds*: rain forest in Buccament, Cumberland and Wallilibou valleys (St Vincent Parrot); montane forest mainly at Richmond Peak and Colonarie and Perseverence Valleys (Whistling Warbler).

Grenada

Wetlands: Levera Pond, Lake St Antoine, Grand Etang, Calivigny Mangrove Swamps, Point Salines Ponds.
Seabird colonies: Cays off east coast of Grenada.
Endemic birds: dry scrub woodland between Grande Anse village and the Lance aux Epines peninsula (Grenada Dove).

Barbados

Wetlands: Graeme Hall Swamp, Chancery Lane Swamp, Long Pond.

Check-list of the birds of the Eastern Caribbean

	VI	ST CR	SOMB ST-BARTS	SABA NEVIS	RED MONT	ANT BARB	GUA	DOM	MART	ST LU	ST VI	BAD	GREN
GREBES *Podicipedidae*													
Least Grebe *Tachybaptus (=Podiceps) dominicus*	N	✓		N	N		N	a		a	a		
Pied-billed Grebe *Podilymbus podiceps*	N	N	N	N	N	N	N	a	N	a	a	✓	N
SHEARWATERS & PETRELS *Procellariidae*													
Black-capped Petrel *Pterodroma hasitata*	a							N?					
Audubon's Shearwater *Puffinus lherminieri*	N	✓	N	N?	N		N	a	N		a	N	N
Greater Shearwater *Puffinus gravis*	a						a	a	a	a			
Sooty Shearwater *Puffinus griseus*	a							a		a			
STORM PETRELS *Hydrobatidae*													
Wilson's Storm-Petrel *Oceanites oceanicus*	✓	✓	✓	✓			✓	a	✓		a	✓	✓
Leach's Storm-Petrel *Oceanodroma leucorhoa*	✓	✓	✓	✓							a	a	✓
TROPICBIRDS *Phaethonidae*													
White-tailed Tropicbird *Phaethon lepturus*	N	N	N	N	N		N	N	N	N?	N	a	N
Red-billed Tropicbird *Phaethon aethereus*	N	N	N	N	N	N	N	o	N	N?	N?	✓	N
BOOBIES & GANNETS *Sulidae*													
Masked Booby *Sula dactylatra*	N	(✓)	N	o	N	o	N	o	N	o	✓	o	N
Brown Booby *Sula leucogaster*	N	✓	N	N		✓		N		✓	N	a	N
Red-footed Booby *Sula sula*	N	(✓)	o	o	N		N	o	N	o	N	a	N

141

	VI	ST CR	SOMB/ST BARTS	SABA/NEVIS	RED/MONT	ANT/BARB	GUA	DOM	MART	ST LU	ST VI	BAD	GREN
PELICANS *Pelecanidae*													
American White Pelican *Pelicanus erythrorhynchus*	a?		a			a?							
Brown Pelican *Pelicanus occidentalis*	N	N	N	N	✓	N	o	✓	o	o?	✓	o	✓
CORMORANTS *Phalacrocoracidae*													
Double-crested Cormorant *Phalacrocorax auritus*	a	a	a?										
Olivaceous Cormorant *Phalacrocorax olivaceus*	a	a	a				a	a		a			a
FRIGATEBIRDS *Fregatidae*													
Magnificent Frigatebird *Fregata magnificens*	N	✓	✓	N	N	N	✓	✓	✓	✓	✓	✓	N
HERONS & BITTERNS *Ardeidae*													
American Bittern *Botaurus lentiginosus*	a	a											
Least Bittern *Ixobrychus exilis*	✓	(✓)											
Great Blue Heron *Ardea herodias*	N	N?			a		o					a	✓
Grey Heron *Ardea cinerea*				✓	✓	✓	N	✓	✓	✓		a	
Great Egret *Casmerodius (Egretta) albus*	N	N	N	✓	✓	✓	✓	✓	✓	✓	✓	✓	
Little Egret *Egretta garzetta*	N	N	N	✓	✓	✓	N	✓	✓	✓	✓	a	
Snowy Egret *Egretta thula*	N	N	N	✓	✓	✓		✓	a	a	o	✓	
Western Reef Heron *Egretta gularis*							N?	N	✓	✓		a	
Little Blue Heron *Egretta caerulea*	N	N	✓	N	N	N	✓	o	✓	a	N	✓	N
Tricolored Heron *Egretta tricolor*	N	✓	o	✓	✓	✓	✓	a	✓	N	a	✓	
Reddish Egret *Egretta rufescens*	a	a	o	o	o					o			
Cattle Egret *Bubulcus ibis*	N	N	N	N	N	N	N	N	N	N	N	N	N

142

	VI	ST CR	SOMB ST BARTS	SABA NEVIS	RED MONT	ANT BARB	GUA	DOM	MART	ST LU	ST VI	BAD	GREN
Green-backed Heron *Butorides striatus*	N	N	N	N	N	N	N	N	N	N	N	N	N
Black-crowned Night Heron *Nycticorax nycticorax*	N	✓	a	N	N	✓	✓	a	✓	o	a	✓	✓
Yellow-crowned Night Heron *Nycticorax violacea*	N	N	N	N	N	N	N	N	N	N	N	✓	N
IBISES & SPOONBILLS *Threskiornithidae*													
White Ibis *Eudocimus albus*	✓							a				a	
Scarlet Ibis *Eudocimus ruber*		a						a?					✓
Glossy Ibis *Plegadis falcinellus*	o			o		o		a	o	a		a	
Roseate Spoonbill *Ajaia ajaia*	a	a	a		✓	o	✓	a					
SWANS, GEESE & DUCKS *Anatidae*													
Fulvous Whistling-Duck *Dendrocygna bicolor*	a	a	o			N	✓	a	o	a	a	o	a
West Indian Whistling-Duck *Dendrocygna arborea*	a	(✓)				N		a?	o	a		a	o
Black-bellied Whistling-Duck *Dendrocygna autumnalis*	a	a	o				a	a	o	a	a	o	a
Green-winged Teal *Anas crecca*	✓	a	o		✓	✓	o	a	o	a	a	o	o
Mallard *Anas platyrhynchos*		✓	o			a?	o	✓	o	a	✓	✓	a
White-cheeked Pintail *Anas bahamensis*	N	a	o			N	o	a?	o			o	o
Northern Pintail *Anas acuta*	N	N	N				o		o	a	a	a	
Blue-winged Teal *Anas discors*	✓	✓	✓	✓	✓	✓	✓	✓	✓	✓	✓	✓	
Cinnamon Teal *Anas cyanoptera*	✓	✓										a	
Eurasian Wigeon *Anas penelope*	✓	a				a						a	✓

143

	VI	ST CR	SOMB-ST BARTS	SABA-NEVIS	RED-MONT	ANT-BARB	GUA	DOM	MART	ST LU	ST VI	BAD	GREN
Northern Shoveler *Anas clypeata*	o	o	o				√	a	o		o?	a	o
American Wigeon *Anas americana*	√	√	o				o		o	o		o	o
Ring-necked Duck *Aythya collaris*	o	o	o			o	o		o	a		o	o
Greater Scaup *Athya marila*		a		√								a	
Lesser Scaup *Aythya affinis*	√	√	√			o	o	a	o	a		o	o
Hooded Merganser *Lophodytes* (= *Mergus*) *cucullatus*	a	a						a	a				
Red-breasted Merganser *Mergus serrator*	a	a				a				a		a	N
Ruddy Duck *Oxyura jamaicensis*	√	o				a		a	N	a	o	a	a
Masked Duck *Nomonyx* (= *oxyura*) *dominica*	a	a				a	N			oN			
OSPREYS *Pandionidae*													
Osprey *Pandion haliaetus*	√	√/aN	√	√	√?	√	√	√	√	√/aN	o	√	√
HAWKS & EAGLES *Accipitridae*													
Hook-billed Kite *Chondrohierax uncinatus*	√	o	o										
Northern Harrier (Marsh Hawk) *Circus cyaneus*						a						a	N
Common Black-Hawk (Crab Hawk) *Buteogallus anthracinus*				a				o	N	a	N		o
Broad-winged Hawk *Buteo platypterus*				N						N	N		a
Red-tailed Hawk *Buteo jamaicensis*	N	N	N			N		N	N	a		a	N
FALCONS & CARACARAS *Falconidae*													
American Kestrel *Falco sparverius*	N	N	N	N	N	√	N	N	N	N	a	a	
Merlin *Falco columbarius*	√	√	√	o	a?	a	√	√	√	o	a	o	o
Peregrine Falcon *Falco peregrinus*	√	√	√	√	o	√	√?	√/aN	√?	o	a	a	o

	VI	ST CR	SOMB-ST BARTS	SABA-NEVIS	RED-MONT	ANT-BARB	GUA	DOM	MART	ST LU	ST VI	BAD	GREN
CURASSOWS, GUANS & CHACHALACAS *Cracidae*													
Rufous-vented Chachalaca *Ortalis ruficauda*													N
PHEASANTS, PARTRIDGES & QUAILS *Phasianidae*													
Northern Bobwhite *Colinus virginianus*	IN	IN											
GUINEA-FOWL *Numididae*													
Helmeted Guinea-Fowl *Numida meleagris*	IN	IN				IN							
RAILS, GALLINULES & COOTS *Rallidae*													
Clapper Rail *Rallus longirostris*	N	N		a		N	N					a	
Sora *Porzana carolina*	✓	✓	✓	✓	✓	✓	✓	✓	✓	o?		✓	✓
Purple Gallinule *Porphyrula martinica*	a	a	o	o?	o	a	N	a?	✓	a?	a	o	✓
Common Moorhen *Gallinula chloropus*	N	N	N	N	N	N	N	N	N	N	a?	N	N
American Coot *Fulica americana*	✓	✓	✓	✓		✓	✓		✓		a	o	o
Caribbean Coot *Fulica caribaea*	N	N	oN		N	N	a	a?	N	a		o	N
PLOVERS & TURNSTONES *Charadriidae*													
Black-bellied Plover *Pluvialis squatarola*	✓	✓	✓	✓	✓	✓	✓	✓	✓	✓	o?	✓	✓
Lesser Golden-Plover *Pluvialis dominica*	✓	✓	a		✓	✓	✓	✓	✓	✓	o	✓	o
Collared Plover *Charadrius collaris*			a	a								a	
Snowy Plover *Charadrius alexandrinus*	N	✓	N	✓		✓				a?		a	✓

	VI	ST CR	SOMB ST BARTS	SABA NEVIS	RED MONT	ANT BARB	GUA	DOM	MART	ST LU	ST VI	BAD	GREN
Wilson's Plover *Charadrius wilsonia*	N	N	N	√	√	N				a?		a	a
Semipalmated Plover *Charadrius semipalmatus*	√	√	√	√	√	√	√	√	√	√	√?	√	√
Piping Plover *Charadrius melodus*	√	o		o		a?						a	
Killdeer *Charadrius vociferus*	N	N	√	o	o	a	o	o	o	a	a	√	
OYSTERCATCHERS *Haematopidae*													
American Oystercatcher *Haematopus palliatus*	N	√	N?		a	a	o		o			a	o
AVOCETS & STILTS *Recurvirostridae*													
Black-necked Stilt *Himantopus mexicanus*	N	N	N	N	o	N	o	o	o	o	o	a	o
American Avocet *Recurvirostra americana*	a	a										a	
WOODCOCK, SNIPE & SANDPIPERS *Scolopacidae*													
Greater Yellowlegs *Tringa melanoleuca*	√	√	√	√	√	√	√	√	√	√	√	√	√
Lesser Yellowlegs *Tringa flavipes*	√	√	√	√	√	√	√	√	√	√	√	√	√
Willet *Catoptrophorus semipalmatus*	N	N	√	√	√?	N	√	o	o	o	a	√	√
Spotted Sandpiper *Actitis macularia*	√	√	√	√	√	√	√	√	√	√	√	√	√
Solitary Sandpiper *Tringa solitaria*	√	√	√	√	√	√	√	√	√	√	√	√	√
Upland Sandpiper *Bartramia longicauda*	√	√	√		√		o	o	o	o?	o?	√	√
Whimbrel *Numenius phaeopus*	√	√	√	o	√	√	√	√	√	o	o	√	√
Long-billed Curlew *Numenius americanus*		a				a?						a	√

146

Species	VI	ST CR	SOMB-ST BARTS	SABA-NEVIS	RED MONT	ANT BARB	GUA	DOM	MART	ST LU	ST VI	BAD	GREN
Marbled Godwit *Limosa fedoa*	a	a		a			a?		a?			a	a
Hudsonian Godwit *Limosa haemastica*	a	a				a	a	a?	a			a	
Black-tailed Godwit *Limosa limosa*	a			a									
Ruddy Turnstone *Arenaria interpres*	✓	✓	✓	✓	✓	✓	✓	✓	✓	✓	✓	✓	✓
Red Knot *Calidris canutus*	a	o	o	lo	✓	✓	a	a	a	a		✓	o
Sanderling *Calidris alba*	o	o	o	o	o?	o	o	o	o	o	✓	✓	✓
Semipalmated Sandpiper *Calidris pusilla*	✓	✓	✓	✓	✓	✓	✓	✓	✓	✓	✓	✓	✓
Western Sandpiper *Calidris mauri*	✓	✓	✓	✓?	✓?	✓	✓	✓	✓	✓	✓	✓	✓
Least Sandpiper *Calidris minutilla*	✓	✓	✓	✓	✓	✓	✓	✓	✓	✓	✓	✓	✓
White-rumped Sandpiper *Calidris fuscicollis*	✓	✓	✓	o	✓	✓	✓	✓	✓		a	✓	✓
Baird's Sandpiper *Calidris bairdii*	✓	o				✓		o				a	
Pectoral Sandpiper *Calidris melanotos*	✓	✓	✓	✓1	✓	✓	✓	✓	✓	✓	✓	✓	✓
Dunlin *Calidris alpina*	a	a				a		a		a	a?	a	o
Curlew Sandpiper *Calidris ferruginea*								a				a	o
Stilt Sandpiper *Calidris (=Micropalama) himantopus*	✓	✓	✓	✓	✓	✓	✓	✓	✓	✓	✓	✓	✓
Buff-breasted Sandpiper *Tryngites subruficollis*		a	a			a	a		a	a	a	✓	a
Ruff *Philomachus pugnax*	a	a					a		a?	a	a	✓	✓
Short-billed Dowitcher *Limnodromus griseus*	✓	✓	✓	✓	o	✓	✓	✓	✓	✓	o	✓	✓
Long-billed Dowitcher *Limnodromus scolopaceus*					✓								
Common Snipe *Gallinago gallinago*	o	o				✓	o	o	o		o?	a	o?
Wilson's Phalarope *Phalaropus tricolor*	✓	✓	✓	✓			a	a	a			✓	✓
Red Phalarope *Phalaropus fulicaria*		a				a						a	a

147

	VI	ST CR	SOMB-ST BARTS	SABA-NEVIS	RED-MONT	ANT-BARB	GUA	DOM	MART	ST LU	ST VI	BAD	GREN
SKUAS & JAEGERS *Stercorariidae*													
Pomarine Skua *Stercorarius pomarinus*	a	a	o	o			o?	✓	o	o	o?	o	o
Arctic Skua *Stercorarius parasiticus*	a	a	a			a		a		a	a	a	a
Long-tailed Skua *Stercorarius longicaudus*	a								a			a	
Skua species *Catharacta skua/maccormicki*	a						a					a	
GULLS & TERNS *Laridae*													
Laughing Gull *Larus atricilla*	N	✓	N	✓	✓	N	✓	✓	✓	✓	✓	✓	N
Black-headed Gull *Larus ridibundus*	a	a	a			a	a	a		a		o	a
Bonaparte's Gull *Larus philadelphia*	o	o	o	a					a	a	a	a	
Ring-billed Gull *Larus delawarensis*	o	o	a	a				a	a	a		a	
Herring Gull *Larus argentatus*		a	a			a?		a				a	
Lesser Black-backed Gull *Larus fuscus*			a		a			a				a	
Great Black-backed Gull *Larus marinus*	N	✓	N	a		o	o	o	o			o	
Gull-billed Tern *Sterna (=Gelochelidon) nilotica*	a	✓		N	N?	a?	✓	a	✓	a		a	a
Caspian Tern *Sterna (=Hydroprogne) caspia*	N	✓	N	✓	✓	✓	N	✓	✓	✓	✓	o	N?
Royal Tern *Sterna maxima*	N	o	N	✓	✓?	✓	N	o	✓	✓	✓	a	✓
Sandwich Tern *Sterna sandvicensis*	N	o	N	✓	✓?	N	N	✓	N	N?	o	o	N
Roseate Tern *Sterna dougallii*	N?	o	N	✓	a	✓	✓	o	✓	✓	✓	a	✓
Common Tern *Sterna hirundo*	a	a				N		✓	✓			a	
Forster's Tern *Sterna forsteri*	a	a			a	✓		✓				✓	
Arctic Tern *Sterna paradisaea*	a	N	N	N	✓	N	N	N	N	✓	✓	✓	N
Least Tern *Sterna antillarum*	N	✓	N	N	N	(✓)	N	N	N	N?	✓	✓	N
Bridled Tern *Sterna anaethetus*	N	✓	N	✓	✓?	N	N	N	N	N?	✓	o	N
Sooty Tern *Sterna fuscata*	N	✓	N	✓		N							

148

Species	VI	ST CR	SOMB-ST-BARTS	SABA-NEVIS	RED-MONT	ANT-BARB	GUA	DOM	MART	ST LU	ST VI	BAD	GREN
Black Tern *Chlidonias niger*	o					o	o	a				a	a
Brown Noddy *Anous stolidus*	N	✓	N	N	N	N	N	N	N	N?	N?	o	N
Black Noddy *Anous minutus*	a		aN					a					
Black Skimmer *Rynchops niger*	a						a						a

PIGEONS & DOVES Columbidae

Species	VI	ST CR	SOMB-ST-BARTS	SABA-NEVIS	RED-MONT	ANT-BARB	GUA	DOM	MART	ST LU	ST VI	BAD	GREN
Rock Dove (Feral Pigeon) *Columba livia*	IN	IN				IN		IN		IN		IN	
Scaly-naped or Red-necked Pigeon *Columba squamosa*	N	N	N	N	N	N	oN	N	oN	N	N	N	N
White-crowned Pigeon *Columba leucocephala*	N*	N	N	o	a	N	oN	a?	a	a		N	
Mourning Dove *Zenaida macroura*	N*												
White-winged Dove *Zenaida asiatica*	N	a	N	N	N		oN	N	oN	N		N	
Zenaida Dove *Zenaida aurita*		N			N	N	a	a	a	N	a	a	N
Eared Dove *Zenaida auriculata*											N?		N
Spotted Dove *Streptopelia chinensis*		IN											
Common Ground-Dove *Columbina passerina*	N	N	N	N	N	N	N	N	N	N	N	N	N
Grenada Dove *Leptotila wellsi*													N
Key West Quail-Dove *Geotrygon chrysia*	N*												
Bridled Quail-Dove *Geotrygon mystacea*	N		✓	N	N	N?	N	(N)	N	(N)		N	N
Ruddy Quail-Dove *Geotrygon montana*	o	N					N	N	N	N	N	N	N

PARROTS, PARAKEETS & MACAWS
Psittacidae

Species	VI	ST CR	SOMB-ST-BARTS	SABA-NEVIS	RED-MONT	ANT-BARB	GUA	DOM	MART	ST LU	ST VI	BAD	GREN
Brown-throated Parakeet *Aratinga pertinax*	IN							IN				IN	

	VI	ST CR	SOMB ST BARTS	SABA NEVIS	RED MONT	ANT BARB	GUA	DOM	MART	ST LU	ST VI	BAD	GREN
Red-necked Parrot *Amazona arausiaca*								N					
St Lucia Parrot *Amazona versicolor*										N			
St Vincent Parrot *Amazona guildingii*											N		
Imperial Parrot *Amazona imperialis*								N					
CUCKOOS & ANIS *Cuculidae*													
Yellow-billed Cuckoo *Coccyzus americanus*	✓	N	✓	✓		✓	a	✓	✓	a?	a	✓	
Mangrove Cuckoo *Coccyzus minor*	N	N	N	✓	N	N	N	N	N	N	N		N
Puerto Rican Lizard Cuckoo *Saurothera vieilloti*	a												
Smooth-billed Ani *Crotophaga ani*	N	N		N	N	a	N	N	a	N	N		N
BARN OWLS *Tytonidae*													
Barn Owl *Tyto alba*								N			N		N
TYPICAL OWLS *Strigidae*													
Puerto Rican Screech Owl *Otus nudipes*	(N)	(N)	a										
Short-eared Owl *Asio flammeus*	a												
NIGHTJARS *Caprimulgidae*													
Common Nighthawk *Chordeiles minor*	✓	✓	o	o	o	o	o	o	o	o?	o?	✓	o?
Antillean Nighthawk *Chordeiles gundlachii*	N	N	?	?	?	?	?	?	?	?	?	?	?
Chuck-will's-widow *Caprimulgus carolinensis*	✓	✓	a	a	a	a							
St Lucia Nightjar *Caprimulgus otiosus*										N			
White-tailed Nightjar *Caprimulgus cayennensis*									N			N	

	VI	ST CR	SOMB-ST BARTS	SABA-NEVIS	RED-MONT	ANT-BARB	GUA	DOM	MART	ST LU	ST VI	BAD	GREN
SWIFTS *Apodidae*													
Black Swift *Cypseloides niger*	a	a	a?	✓	N	✓	N	N	N	N	N	✓	o
White-collared Swift *Streptoprocne zonaris*	a			a									a
Short-tailed Swift *Chaetura brachyura*		a											
Gray-rumped Swift *Chaetura cinereiventris*													N
Lesser Antillean Swift *Chaetura martinica*					a		N	N	N	N	N		
Chimney Swift *Chaetura pelagica*	a	a										a	
HUMMINGBIRDS *Trochilidae*													
Rufous-breasted Hermit *Glaucis hirsuta*	N												N
Antillean Mango *Anthracothorax dominicus*	a	a		a									
Purple-throated Carib *Eulampis jugularis*				N	N	N	N	N	N	N	N	a	a
Green-throated Carib *Sericotes holosericeus*	N	N	N	N	N	N	N	N	N	N	N	N	N
Antillean Crested Hummingbird *Orthorhyncus cristatus*	N	N	N	N	N	N	N	N	N	N	N	N	N
Blue-headed Hummingbird *Cyanophaia bicolor*								N	N				
KINGFISHERS *Alcedinidae*													
Ringed Kingfisher *Ceryle torquata*					✓		N	N				✓	
Belted Kingfisher *Ceryle alcyon*	✓	✓	✓	✓	✓	✓	✓	✓	✓	✓	✓	✓	✓
WOODPECKERS, PICULETS & WRYNECKS *Picidae*													
Puerto Rican Woodpecker *Melanerpes portoricensis*	N*												

151

	VI	ST CR	SOMB-ST BARTS	SABA-NEVIS	RED-MONT	ANT-BARB	GUA	DOM	MART	ST LU	ST VI	BAD	GREN
Guadeloupe Woodpecker *Melanerpes herminieri*							N						
Yellow-bellied Sapsucker *Sphyrapicus varius*	✓	✓	a			a?		a					
TYRANT FLYCATCHERS Tyrannidae													
Caribbean Elaenia *Elaenia martinica*	N	N	N	N	N	N	N	N	N	N	N	N	N
Yellow-bellied Elaenia *Elaenia flavogaster*					N						N		N
Euler's Flycatcher *Empidonax euleri*		a										a	(✓)
Eastern Wood Pewee *Contopus virens*							N	N	N				
Lesser Antillean Pewee *Contopus latirostris*				N						N			N
Grenada Flycatcher *Myiarchus nugator*											N		N
Puerto Rican Flycatcher *Myiarchus antillarum*	N												
Lesser Antillean Flycatcher *Myiarchus oberi*		a		N	N	N	N	N	N	N			
Tropical Kingbird *Tyrannus melancholicus*													(N)
Loggerhead Kingbird *Tyrannus caudifasciatus*	N*		N										
Gray Kingbird *Tyrannus dominicensis*	N	N	a	N	N	N	N	N	N	N	N	N	N
Fork-tailed Flycatcher *Tyrannus savana*	N			o								o	✓
SWALLOWS Hirundinidae													
Purple Martin *Progne subis*	N	aN											
Caribbean Martin *Progne dominicensis*	N	N	N	N	N	N	N	N	N	N	N?	N	N
Tree Swallow *Tachycineta (= Iridoprocne) bicolor*	a	a											
Northern Rough-winged Swallow *Stelgidopteryx serripennis*	a	a	✓	o			✓	✓	✓	a	a		
Bank Swallow *Riparia riparia*	o	o			?	?						✓	

	GREN	BAD	ST VI	ST LU	MART	DOM	GUA	ANT-BARB	RED-MONT	SABA-NEVIS	SOMB-ST BARTS	ST CR	VI
Cliff Swallow *Hirundo pyrrhonota*		✓	a	a		o		a?		a	a	✓	✓
Barn Swallow *Hirundo rustica*	✓	✓	✓	✓	✓	✓	✓	✓	✓	✓	✓	✓	✓
Cave Swallow *Hirundo (= Petrochelidon) fulva*			a	a								a	o
WRENS *Troglodytidae*													
House Wren *Troglodytes aedon*	N		N	N	(N)	N	(N)						
MUSCICAPIDS *Muscicapidae*													
Subfamily SOLITAIRES, THRUSHES and ALLIES *Turdinae*													
Rufous-throated Solitaire *Myadestes genibarbis*				N	N	N				a			a
Veery *Catharus fuscescens*													
Cocoa Thrush *Turdus fumigatus*	N		N	N	N								
Bare-eyed Thrush *Turdus nudigensis*	N		N			N							
Red-legged Thrush *Turdus plumbeus*						N							
Forest Thrush *Cichlherminia lherminieri*				N			N		N				
MOCKINGBIRDS & THRASHERS *Mimidae*													
Northern Mockingbird *Mimus polyglottos*												N	N
Tropical Mockingbird *Mimus gilvus*	N		N	N	N	N	N			o			
White-breasted Thrasher *Ramphocinclus brachyurus*				N	N								
Scaly-breasted Thrasher *Margarops fuscus*		N	N	N	N	N	N	N	N	N	N	N	N
Pearly-eyed Thrasher *Margarops fuscatus*	(N)	a	(a)	N	N	N	N	N	N	N	N	N	N
Trembler *Cinclocerthia ruficauda*			N	N	N	N	N	a?	N	N			a

153

	VI	ST CR	SOMB ST BARTS	SABA NEVIS	RED MONT	ANT BARB	GUA	DOM	MART	ST LU	ST VI	BAD	GREN
WAXWINGS *Bombycillidae*													
Cedar Waxwing *Bombycilla cedrorum*	a						a	a	a				a
STARLINGS and ALLIES *Sturnidae*													
European Starling *Sturnus vulgaris*		a											
VIREOS *Vireonidae*													
White-eyed Vireo *Vireo griseus*	a												
Yellow-throated Vireo *Vireo flavifrons*	o	a											
Red-eyed Vireo *Vireo olivaceus*	a	a				a	a	a		a	a	a	a
Black-whiskered Vireo *Vireo altiloquus*	N	N	N	N	N	N	N	N	N	N	N	N	N
EMBERIZIDS *Emberizidae*													
Subfamily WOOD WARBLERS *Parulinae*													
Blue-winged Warbler *Vermivora pinus*	o	a	a										
Tennessee Warbler *Vermivora peregrina*	a	✓	✓	✓	✓	✓	✓	✓	✓	o	o	✓	o
Northern Parula *Parula americana*	N	N	N	N	N	N	N	N	N	N	✓	N	√/N
Yellow Warbler *Dendroica petechia*	o	o		a		a	a	a			a	a	
Chestnut-sided Warbler *Dendroica pensylvanica*	o	a	a	a		o	a	a					
Magnolia Warbler *Dendroica magnolia*	o	a	a		a	o	a	a	a	a	a	a	o
Cape May Warbler *Dendroica tigrina*	✓	✓	a	o		o	a	a				o	
Black-throated Blue Warbler *Dendroica caerulescens*	✓	✓	a	o	a	o	a	a	a		a	a	o

Species	GREN	BAD	ST VI	ST LU	MART	DOM	GUA	ANT-BARB	RED-MONT	SABA-NEVIS	SOMB-ST-BARTS	ST CR	VI
Yellow-rumped (Myrtle) Warbler *Dendroica coronata*		o		o	o	o	o	a		a	o	✓	✓
Black-throated Green Warbler *Dendroica virens*	a	a				a		a		a		o	a?
Blackburnian Warbler *Dendroica fusca*		a				a	a		a			o	o
Yellow-throated Warbler *Dendroica dominica*				N				N?	a	✓	✓		o
Adelaide's Warbler *Dendroica adelaidae*								a				✓	N
Prairie Warbler *Dendroica discolor*	o	a			o							o	✓
Palm Warbler *Dendroica palmarum*												a	o
Bay-breasted Warbler *Dendroica castanea*		a				a		a?				a	a
Blackpoll Warbler *Dendroica striata*	✓	✓		✓	✓	✓	✓	a	✓	✓	o	✓	✓
Plumbeous Warbler *Dendroica plumbea*						N	N						
Whistling Warbler *Catharopeza bishopi*			N										
Black-and-white Warbler *Mniotilta varia*			✓	✓?	✓	✓	✓	✓	✓	✓	✓	✓	✓
American Redstart *Setophaga ruticilla*	✓	✓	✓	✓	✓	✓	✓	✓	✓	✓	✓	✓	✓
Prothonotary Warbler *Protonotaria citrea*	✓	✓		o?	o	✓	o	o?	o?	o	o	o	o
Worm-eating Warbler *Helmitheros vermivorus*		✓					o	a			a	o	✓
Swainson's Warbler *Limnothlypis swainsonii*													a
Ovenbird *Seiurus aurocapillus*		a	a?	o?	✓	✓	✓	o	✓	✓	✓	✓	✓
Northern Waterthrush *Seiurus noveboracensis*	✓	✓	a?	o?	✓	✓	✓	✓	✓	✓	✓	✓	✓
Louisiana Waterthrush *Seiurus motacilla*	✓	a	a?		o	a	o	a	o	o	a	✓	✓
Kentucky Warbler *Oporornis formosus*							o	o?			a		o
Connecticut Warbler *Oporornis agilis*											a		a?
Common Yellowthroat *Geothlypis trichas*						a		a				o	o

155

	VI	ST CR	SOMB-ST BARTS	SABA-NEVIS	RED-MONT	ANT-BARB	GUA	DOM	MART	ST LU	ST VI	BAD	GREN
Semper's Warbler *Leucopeza semperi*										(N)			
Hooded Warbler *Wilsonia citrina*	o	o	a	o		o	o	a	o				
Canada Warbler *Wilsonia canadensis*	a	a					a					N	
Subfamily BANANAQUITS Coerebinae													
Bananaquit *Coereba flaveola*	N	N	N	N	N	N	N	N	N	N	N	N	N
Subfamily TANAGERS Thraupinae													
Lesser Antillean Tanager *Tangara cucullata*											N		N
Antillean or Blue-hooded Euphonia *Euphonia musica*			o	N?	N	N	N	N	N	N	N		(N)
Summer Tanager *Piranga rubra*		a		a	a	o		a		a		a	a
Scarlet Tanager *Piranga olivacea*	a	a	a			✓	✓		✓			✓	o
Subfamily CARDINALS, GROSBEAKS and ALLIES Cardinalinae													
Streaked Saltator *Saltator albicollis*	a	a		a			N	N	N	N			
Rose-breasted Grosbeak *Pheucticus ludovicianus*		a				o		o				a	
Blue Grosbeak *Guiraca caerulea*	o												o
Indigo Bunting *Passerina cyanea*	✓	✓		✓									
Subfamily EMBERIZINES Emberizinae													
Blue-black Grassquit *Volatinia jacarina*													N
Yellow-bellied Seedeater *Sporophila nigrocollis*											a		N

	VI	ST CR	SOMB-ST-BARTS	SABA-NEVIS	RED-MONT	ANT-BARB	GUA	DOM	MART	ST LU	ST VI	BAD	GREN
Yellow-faced Grassquit *Tiaris olivacea*	N*	N	N	N	N	N	N	N	N	N	N	N	N
Black-faced Grassquit *Tiaris bicolor*	N	N	N	N	N	N	N	N	N	N	N	N	N
Lesser Antillean Bullfinch *Loxigilla noctis*	N					a	N		N	N	N	N	o
St Lucia Black Finch *Melanospiza richardsoni*										N			
Grassland Yellow Finch *Sicalis luteola*													
Subfamily BLACKBIRDS and ALLIES *Icterinae*													
Bobolink *Dolichonyx oryzivorus*	o	o	o	o			o	o	o			o	o
Greater Antillean Grackle *Quiscalus niger*	N*												
Carib Grackle *Quiscalus lugubris*	N		N	N	N	N	N	N	N	N	N	N	N
Shiny Cowbird *Molothrus bonariensis*									N		N	N	N
St Lucia Oriole *Icterus laudabilis*										N			
Montserrat Oriole *Icterus oberi*					N								
Martinique Oriole *Icterus bonana*									N				
Troupial *Icterus icterus*	IN		a	a		o						a	o
Northern Oriole *Icterus galbula*	o					a		o					o
WEAVERS *Ploceidae*													
Village Weaver *Ploceus cucullatus*		IN					SN		IN				
Red Bishop *Euplectes orix*									I				
ESTRILDID FINCHES *Estrildidae*													
Bronze Mannikin *Lonchura cucullata*	I								I				

157

NOTES

N = Nesting

√ = Present (usually as migrant or winter visitor)

I = Introduced

o = occasional

a = accidental

N?, a? = Present status uncertain

(N), (√) = may no longer nest/occur

* refers to Vieques only

This list follows the order and nomenclature adopted by the American Ornithologists' Union Check-list of North American Birds (1983, 6th edition) which includes the Caribbean region.

Coverage of many islands is very incomplete so with better knowledge, the status of several species is likely to be uprated. Any new information that visitors or residents can provide would be greatly appreciated by the author, and will help to update the list in future editions.

Unestablished exotics, and vagrant species recorded only once this century in the region have been omitted from the list.

Arrangement is geographical by island or island group where they share the same bank (thus St Croix is separated from the rest of the Virgin Islands).

VI = Culebra, Vieques (east of Puerto Rico), St Thomas, St John, Virgin Gorda, Anegada and all their adjacent islands

ST CR = St Croix and its adjacent islands

SOMB-ST BARTS = Sombrero, Dog Island, Anguilla, Saint Martin/Saint Maarten, St Barthelemy and their adjacent islands

SABA-NEVIS = Saba, Saint Eustatius, St Kitts-Nevis

RED-MONT = Redonda, Montserrat

ANT-BARB = Antigua and Barbuda

GUA = Guadeloupe (Grande Terre, Basse Terre, La Desirade, Marie-Galante)

DOM = Dominica

MAR = Martinique

ST LU = St Lucia

ST VI = St Vincent

BAD = Barbados

GREN = Grenada and the Grenadines (Bequia, Mustique, Canouan, Union, Carriacou and adjacent islands)

Index